DESTINY KEEPS CALLING ME

RISING ABOVE LIFE'S TRAIN WRECKS

A MEMOIR

JACKIE DENISE

FOREWORD BY TAMMIE T. HARRIS

DESTINY KEEPS CALLING ME
Rising Above Life's Train Wrecks

JACKIE DENISE
jackiedavent@gmail.com

ISBN 978-1-943342-54-9

Printed in the USA.
All rights reserved

Published by: Destined To Publish | Flossmoor, Illinois
www.DestinedToPublish.com

DEDICATION

First of all, I dedicate this book to God, my Heavenly Father, who has been faithful to me ALL my life: Even today, God, Your unconditional love continues to call my name, for which I am grateful.

Secondly, I dedicate it to my dear daughter, the most beautiful and brilliant butterfly I have ever seen: Marquaysa, God has exceeded my prayers regarding your unique path, and your faith-filled, fierce approach to life never ceases to amaze me! Keep giving life your very best. And may God reward you by continuing to release heaven's best to you.

Love you always.

~Mom (whom you affectionately call "Ms. Jackie")

Thirdly, I dedicate it to every woman who is determined to outlive traumatic train wrecks and become what Destiny has called her to be—nothing less, nothing more, and nothing else.

TABLE OF CONTENTS

FOREWORD

As a 12-year-old junior high student, I met Jackie while dressing out for gym, and she would later become my best friend and sister. Here is a funny story that drew us together: I was asking everyone in the locker room if they knew this new song with the lyrics, "L-A-D-I-E-S are the best, L-A-D-I-E-S are the best..." Jackie was *the only one* in the locker room who knew the song! We immediately started singing it out loud together while dancing around and have done so randomly for more than 40 years.

I've also had the honor of working with Jackie Denise on many occasions in the areas of ministry, health and wellness, mental health, family therapy, and, most recently, mindset coaching. I can tell you that she is "The Real Deal" and magnificent in whatever she does. In her capacity as a Mindset and Deliverance Coach as well as a dynamic preacher, she shares biblical truths to promote activating courage and strength to birth your NEW NEXT.

Addressed are traumatic issues with twists and turns that offer hope for fulfillment of God's promises. You will learn how to avoid unnecessary train wrecks, heal from them, and let go of the shame and pain caused. There will be a demonstration of God's power in forgiving others and yourself for choices and mistakes made.

I affectionally call her "Jack" sometimes, and after reading her book, I now see why! Transparent moments encourage women to get back up again after crashes, falls, and losses when it seems like they cannot. Jackie's ability to rise from difficult and challenging experiences despite being unable to change the past is inspirational to me.

I've walked with Jackie and witnessed her story grow, develop, and change over the years with my very own eyes. I can say, "She has become a Super Shero who has won many battles along the way, and it is simply marvelous!" Past scars are shared with you so that your scars may be healed through her deliverance ministry in story form.

If you want to see what miracles, signs, and wonders look like, read this book, and you will experience exactly that. I certainly did!

Tammie T. Harris

New Seed Ministries Pastor
Real Estate CEO/Coach
Best-Selling Author/Speaker

PREFACE

Although I had adverse childhood experiences, drama, and trauma that persisted into adulthood, I am alive and soaked in God's unmerited grace. Hence, I can share these true stories. A gazillion times, I honestly thought I wouldn't make it, and felt destined to ride the struggle bus all my life. During some periods of my life, I wondered if mindless choices bound me to a belief system that diminished my self-worth and value.

These underdeveloped beliefs sometimes led me to make unwise decisions. It occurred to me that perhaps ungodly confessions ignorantly spoken over me had condemned me to the core. Rather than healthy deposits, ridiculous associations left me with significant psychological and emotional deficits. Occasionally, I wondered whether my ancestors' unrepented actions had cursed me through the bloodline. God's grace helped me survive every thought I couldn't understand. As time passed, I concluded that my life had never been condemned. I had been CHOSEN to be a voice for God's grace and power. With chosenness had come some unavoidable suffering.

That chosenness and my resilient faith have enabled me to rise—repeatedly—from every symptom and type of trauma I have experienced. Consequently, I'm alive today to talk candidly about how God guided me as a teen runaway, abandoned on the streets of New York City with no contact information in my head or money in my pocket. I'm alive to declare how God miraculously healed my body from a health crisis with no known cure. I'm alive to proclaim how He brought my precious baby out of a child abuse-induced coma and confounded the enemy with his radical recovery. I'm alive to tell how God completely reversed the tattered relationship between my dear mama and me and made it as if the past pain had never occurred.

Yes, my living and not prematurely dying were etched into God's perfect plan. I'm alive to share how I survived a violent relationship although two physical scars remain. I'm alive to convey how God sent me to prison to learn how to break free of racial barriers and minister with the heart of Christ. I'm alive to testify how God's love delivered me from a master demonic spirit sent to destroy me.

Many women are experiencing similar or worse traumatic situations. Some of you have wondered if you will ever recover from such a pain-peppered life, and the unresolved trauma stings. It's time to believe again because you are still alive, which means that God is still able! I share these transparent stories of my rising above emotional, physical, and psychological trauma to assure you that you can, will, and must RISE above the obstacles you think are insurmountable.

The cost is high when you don't know who you are and have no clear sense of direction. The presence of this book in your hand at this moment confirms that you're being molded, crushed, and refashioned into something breathtakingly beautiful. God still has an extraordinary plan for your life, so hold on. Take advantage of my transparent mistakes and sometimes unnecessary suffering to learn and grow. Read with a listening heart as you seek motivation, inspiration, transformation, healing, and deliverance. Please allow this transparent download to help you identify red flags and overcome the effects of unresolved trauma: Follow the tracks of my tears and use them to course-correct immediately.

INTRODUCTION

If I could sit down for a quaint dinner with the silly girl I once was, I would say, "Gurl, please! Be easy. You were designed with destiny in mind. No matter what, remember that God has a purpose and a plan, and your purpose is to build up women. Also, believe in yourself because you DO have it in you! Remember your value and worth, for you are absolutely priceless."

Journey with me now through 12 of my most defining "train wreck" stories. "Train wreck" is my metaphor for adverse childhood experiences, drama, and trauma that persist into adulthood as described in these pages that are not strictly chronological. You will see as you read that I. LOVE. WORDS, and I am a self-proclaimed wordsmith! Playing school with friends as a child, I was always the teacher. I took accelerated English classes at an early age, and books were my constant companions. Throughout my schooling, I won spelling bees and oratorical competitions up to the state level. Scrabble is my favorite board game, and I played expertly for decades.

Weekly Toastmasters meetings kept my brain tank full of innovative words that I mastered impromptu. Ministry school taught me how to use alliteration to make my major points more memorable. As a result of my sociological and behavior modification training, I have linked each chapter with traumatic social problems women may experience. The letter "D" bore in my soul since this was a book about deliverance. The other "D's" fell in place like a line of dominoes.

Just as Jesus taught in parables, I teach and coach using metaphors because I also like to keep things simple instead of deep and spooky. I am compelled to break information down into ABC 123 formats so that anyone facing or recovering from a train wreck can understand every word that comes from my mouth. I speak to others what I needed spoken to myself when life events tried to wreck me. God never let the powers of darkness kill me; He always sent a timely word. Sometimes His voice released just one word: "Jackie."

Destiny has never stopped calling my name, and every moment has shaped me into who I am today. Hallelujah! The recurring call stirred me back to life when it seemed the train wrecks would not stop coming. Destiny's call alerted angelic rescuers regarding my location when I was buried under violent, destructive, or self-imposed wreckage.

Sister, if the locomotive you're riding is about to run off the tracks, don't pretend you don't see or know what you KNOW you do.

Activate your faith, and take the action deemed appropriate. Jumping from a runaway train before it hits the guardrail is deemed appropriate. Exiting at the next stop as quickly as possible without grabbing your bags is deemed appropriate. Perhaps an unexplainable, crazy collision has already taken place. Oh my! Finding the courage to rise above life's train wrecks is challenging, but it will be worth it when the smoke clears. If you slip into a deep coma, your spirit will still hear the rescuers calling your name as they dig through the debris. I pray that destiny will call your name and *keep calling* until you answer.

train wreck
noun
trān·rek

1: a violent and destructive crash involving a train
2: an utter disaster or mess: a disastrous
calamity or source of trouble [1]

destined
transitive verb
des·tined

1:1: to decree beforehand: PREDETERMINE

2b: to direct, devise, or set apart for

a specific purpose or place.[2]

CHAPTER 1

DESTINED: ASLEEP INSIDE THE OVEN

Years ago, my Aunt Joann told me that when I was a little girl, the family would look for me before finally finding me asleep inside the oven. I incredulously said, "The OVEN?!" She confirmed that it was the case; however, she could not tell me why I used to do it. Occasionally, I have prayed and asked the Lord for insight into that curious, even dangerous, childhood habit. My professional mental health background convinced me there was more behind the behavior. Perhaps I feared something or someone. Maybe I was as sensitive to the cold then as I am now and sought warmth. I know that these are mere assumptions, but I wasn't sure until today, while I was driving through Rocky Mount.

While in the city, I felt nostalgic about driving by my childhood home at 312 Middle Street. Perhaps looking at the house where

I experienced and caused so much drama would ramp up my writing motor, enabling me to complete this manuscript. As I approached the street, I heard the Holy Spirit whisper, "No, keep going." I obeyed. A forgotten memory dropped onto me just a few blocks away: "You used to be found asleep inside the oven." I was prompted to call my auntie and revisit that conversation.

I listened with purposeful ears this time. Aunt Joann stuck to the story that I would sometimes be found asleep in the oven when I was a baby. She said my Grandma Hattie would keep the oven door open most of the time. Family members would walk by and see me curled up, sleeping inside it like it was a bed.

Aunt Joann told me Grandma Hattie had warned everyone not to close the oven because "Jackie might be in there."

When I asked my aunt why she thought I used to do that, she emphatically said, "I don't know! You must have been cold and trying to get warm. One day, when you tried to climb into the oven, it was hot, and that's how you got that burn on your hand. But after that, you never climbed back into the oven. And nobody told you not to either; you just didn't do it."

After talking with my aunt for a while, I told her how grateful I was that no one had ever closed the oven door and pressed the preheat button with me inside. Laughing, she said with a hint of exasperation, "Jackie! We didn't have preheated ovens back then; the pilot had to be lit."

All I could say while smiling was, "Oh."

As I continued driving up the highway and pondering the situation, I looked down for a moment. If not for the 50-cent-sized burn scar on my left hand that has always been there, I might not have believed her story. It sounded so absurd; common sense was missing from the scenario.

Why would a toddler repeatedly climb into a cold, dark oven and fall asleep? Why didn't my family shut the oven door after seeing me in it the first or second time?! Grandma Hattie was a sharp cookie, so it must have somehow been part of my purpose. Perhaps destiny's call included early exposure to the fiery furnace of affliction. In Isaiah 48:10, God says, *"Behold, I have refined you, but not as silver; I have tried you in the furnace of affliction."* As a toddler, I got badly burned while climbing into a hot oven; I think that prepared me for the fiery path I would follow later with respect to my decisions and choices.

Think about it for a moment: Ovens are enclosed vessels and containers; heated chambers used to slowly roast or bake items at high temperatures until they are thoroughly cooked from the inside out. I smile as I recall Grandma Hattie's homemade biscuits and moist yellow cakes, which I enjoyed as a child. It's almost as if I can taste them as I recall licking the big bowl and spoon clean. Aside from roasting and baking, ovens were used as a source of heat for the home. Aha! Perhaps that's why the door was left open so often.

Many scorching hot situations in life require us to stand on faith even when the outcomes don't seem favorable. Remember how Daniel and his three friends disobeyed King Nebuchadnezzar in chapter 3 of Daniel? I see the divine similarities between their encounter with a furnace and my encounter with the oven with fresh eyes. I wasn't tied up and thrown into the blazing hot oven like the Hebrew boys were tossed into the furnace; I was drawn into it. They weren't completely burned to ashes as the Chaldeans had hoped. Thank God, neither was I. The survival of the Hebrew boys showed God's power in his utter confoundment of the enemy and everyone who expected to see a cremation on that fateful day. My survival with only a dim scar confirms the same!

Testing in the furnace of affliction is for the called & the chosen.

deserted
adjective
de·sert·ed

1: to withdraw from or usually leave
without intent to return
2 a: to leave in the lurch[1]

CHAPTER 2

DESERTED: ALONE IN A BRONX COURTYARD

My naturally curious and willful nature made growing up with an authoritarian parent challenging. The old saying goes, "A hard head makes a soft tail!" It isn't that discreet, but you get the drift, right? In my home, refusing to listen and to obey the iron-fist rules to the letter was not an option. Therefore, I found myself in hot water at the age of 14 years. I'm talking about boiling water!

Being the oldest and taking care of my siblings while Mama worked was a lot of responsibility, and I didn't want it. I watched over them, but not hanging out with my friends made me mad. I was even angrier because everyone else was still out having fun, while I had to be in the house before dark. Every day, I was beyond annoyed when my mama said, "I'm heading to work now; nobody in and nobody out!" I felt deprived a lot of the time and like I was in solitary confinement with an 11-year-old and a four-year-old while my friends were free. It sucked, so I broke the rules over and over again. Despite my mama's warnings, I often let my friends in as soon as her black Pontiac turned the corner. It was so much fun dancing, listening to music, and eating all the snacks until . . . the night mama showed up unexpectedly! She cleared the crowd out, grounded me, and double-dog dared me to open her front door again without permission.

Thanks to Edwards Junior High School, I could stay in touch with my friends. That was cool until it suddenly wasn't. I will never forget the day a well-known girl gang member saw me talking to her boyfriend in the cafeteria and thought I was "trying to get her man." It was the furthest thing from the truth. We were just discussing class, but she refused to believe it. She pointed at me then beat her fist into her palm and said, "I'm gonna beat your black *** after school!" I thought she was just talking smack to be cool or to show off, but she was extremely serious. Unfortunately, we lived in the same neighborhood and rode the same bus. The moment I stepped off the bottom step of the bus at the bus stop, she and her friend jumped on me like white on rice. Everyone crowded around like they were at the newest movie premiere. Not one person helped me. Instead, they pointed and laughed as they watched the show. All that was missing was buttered popcorn.

Those two gang girls were notorious bullies, and their crew was known for causing severe damage in the community. I was physically and psychologically wounded by their actions on that day. They beat me to a pulp over something stupid that had never even happened. The right side of my face still bears a faint scar where one of those fools bit into my jaw, causing it to swell like it did when I had the mumps at the age of 10 years. I made it home bloodied. I was barely able to see or walk straight from the pain I felt all over.

Mama didn't exclaim with rage over my battered condition, hold me, or help clean me up. All I wanted was a hug. However, I knew better than to ask her for one or even approach her. Giving hugs and kisses was simply not Mama's love language. She drove me straight to the magistrate's office to file a complaint, but nothing came of it—nothing except that I became terrified of leaving the house for fear of being jumped again and beaten worse.

I tried to explain my fear to Mama. She didn't want to hear about it. When I told her that those girls were still out there, she reiterated that she did not want to listen to me talking about my fears. My mama said I had to go outside, or *she* would beat me next. I felt I had no one to protect me. They say, "If you can't beat them, join them." So I joined the gang out of a sense of self-preservation. As a result of this decision, I adopted their tough outward appearance. There was nothing authentic or genuine about it. Because I felt I had no choice, I became somewhat of a menace to society right alongside them. It worked for a while until one day, a light bulb started flickering furiously in my head.

A female student whose name escapes me was touring Edwards Junior High School. As she passed me in the hallway, she heard someone loudly call out my birth name, Jackie Crandall. I answered and dapped the girl up. The new student stood there, staring at me with her mouth wide open. She said, "Oh my God, *you're* Jackie Crandall?! You're THE Jackie Crandall?!" I confirmed my identity with a slight head nod. With her hand raised to her mouth and in an astonished voice, the girl said, "I've heard about you! I'm coming to this school next year. I want to be down with you, so can we please be friends? I don't want to have any trouble when I transfer!"

I remember cocking my head to the side and squinting my eyes in disbelief. I tried to take in what she had just said. Yeah, I had heard right, and it stunned me. The realization that I was perpetrating a horrible fraud gut-punched me. Unknowingly, she had pulled back the curtains on the facade I had created solely to meet my self-preservation needs. The fake reputation I had developed had preceded me to the point where someone wanted to be my "friend" for protection, not for true friendship's sake. Not because I was a fantastic, fun person but because they feared physical harm from me. Not because I was just me but because they feared what I might one day do to them or take from them. Looking at myself through her eyes made me realize that the fighting, boosting, hell-raising way I'd adopted was a disappointing dead-end. I recognized that I was just a great pretender. I cut ties with the gang the same day. Thankfully, they let me go without a fight.

Unfortunately, I was still fighting for more freedom at home against my mama's emotionally detached, authoritarian parenting style. It was what she had learned and knew, so it was what she gave. Her favorite answers seemed to be "No," "My way or the highway," "Don't ask me no questions," and "Because I said so." A disaster was waiting to happen to this girl, who felt unloved and was looking for love everywhere. At that time, I considered myself to be in love with my boyfriend and sneaked around and had sex with him whenever possible. We sometimes skipped school to listen to new music, write rap lyrics, or sharpen our turntable skills. Back then, some of my favorite artists were Run-DMC, Doug E. Fresh, Rob Base & DJ E-Z Rock, Salt-N-Pepa, Roxanne Shanté, Eric B. & Rakim, Slick Rick, and Big Daddy Kane. Oh, my goodness! I especially loved mixing Run-DMC, Salt-N-Pepa, and Roxanne Shanté. Creating a brand-new sound felt incredible, and I would mix the albums on my two turntables until my wrists hurt.

Another pastime of mine was shoplifting, which I had done often with the gang. I did it even more on my own. I was so good at it that I thought I was invincible, became greedy, and finally got caught. The item that I ended up in court over was a pair of pretty little white shoes with flower bows on top and kitten heels. I had stolen the first pair from Shoe Show on Sunset Avenue, close to City Lake. I had gotten away with the theft but liked them so much that when they wore out, I audaciously went back to the store and stole another pair exactly like them. I got stopped after exiting the store. Now, how dumb was that? When my court date arrived, it was such an embarrassing nightmare that I swore I'd never shoplift again.

Even though I had decided to straighten up, Mama seemed to be fed up with my mess. I overheard her and my grandmother talking. I heard the words "DSS" and "training school." I realized I was getting into trouble but decided right then and there that I wasn't THAT doggone bad! Therefore, I was not going to go to anybody's training school!

After hearing what I heard, I spent the next few days trying to figure out what to do. Mama, however, moved faster than I expected. I arrived home from school one day, and shortly after, a middle-aged Black lady appeared at the front door. She was dark-skinned like me and wearing lipstick that wasn't quite red. It was more of a burnt sienna color, and I thought it looked very pretty on her. She said to me, "Hi, Jackie. I'm Mrs. Arlene. You and I are going on a little ride."

A little ride?! Mama acted like she didn't see the confused look on my face. She waved her hand in the air and said two words: "Go on." I received no further explanation from either of them.

Hesitantly, I got into Mrs. Arlene's white government car, and we drove away.

Although I was never told where I was going, the words "DSS" and "training school" kept replaying in my head. After a little while, my adolescent mind replaced those words with my own: "But I'm not going!" That thought became louder and louder with every minute that I sat in the front passenger seat. I will NEVER for the life of me understand why Mrs. Arlene stopped at the local Piggly Wiggly grocery store and told me to wait in the car.

Well, you already know what happened. Within seconds of Mrs. Arlene's walking through the door of that store, I bounded out of that impending jail cell like a cannonball and took off running! I ran like Kunta Kinte before they cut off his foot. I did not stop running until I arrived at the cute little green vinyl siding house across the street from the graveyard, where my boyfriend, Arif, lived with his Aunt Mary. I had a positive relationship with Aunt Mary, and we thought highly of each other. I believe it may have been because she talked to me and showed me what I believed to be true interest and love, which I did not feel I received at home.

After I explained what I believed was happening, we devised a plan. Arif was scheduled to go home to New York for a family visit, so he and his aunt decided that he would go immediately and take me with him. While my mama worked the third shift,

I snuck home to get my clothes. Moreover, I shamelessly stole some of Mama's money to pay for my Greyhound bus ticket.

I lay low at Aunt Mary's home for three days then she drove us to the bus station in the middle of the night. There were a million stops during our bus ride, and it was freezing. Upon our arrival in the Big Apple, I had an excruciatingly painful crook in my neck from falling asleep against the bus window. A foolish 14-year-old girl, I was unprepared to recognize that as a warning sign of troubles ahead.

In less than a week, I had become a bona fide runaway. As far as I was concerned, I was not out of control and was saving myself from unknown training school horrors. It is commonly believed that some kids run away because they are hardheaded and don't want to follow the rules. Sometimes parents do not realize that their message can be spot on, but their children will completely miss the point if the methodology for sharing the message is messed up.

At my boyfriend's home in New York, I met his mom Sharon, stepdad Robert, and sister Peanut. Less than a year apart, he and Peanut had grown up incredibly close. She felt threatened when she saw that he cared for me. It was as if I had come between them. That jealous chick hated my guts from the moment she laid her eyes on me, and I am convinced she immediately began brainstorming how to get rid of me. She would not give me half a chance and refused to get to know me. Peanut visited friends regularly for months without inviting me along. I could do or say nothing right in her opinion, and we always argued. She ran her mouth way too much one day. Another significant mistake she made was hitting me, thinking I would back down, but I didn't. We tore up that apartment at 246 West 149th Street in Manhattan, New York! From that day on, it became a war zone where we fought constantly.

Because she was always starting something with me, I remained on guard. One day, Peanut suddenly announced she wanted to call a truce with me. She said she was tired of fighting. She even asked nicely and with a cheerful smile, "Can we please start over and be friends?" In my naive arrogance, I thought it was because the city mouse was tired of a country mouse whooping her tail in at least every other fight.

Even though I was tired of fighting, I didn't have a problem with her—she had a major problem with me. I genuinely *wanted* to be friends, so I welcomed the chance to start over, and we shook hands. Peanut warmly invited me to visit her girlfriends in the Bronx on that day. Wow! I was *so* glad to go out and finally meet them. We got dressed and headed for the train. We had no fare, so Peanut showed me how to train hop without paying. We had to jump over turnstiles quickly without falling, getting stuck, or getting caught. Although I was scared at first, the adrenaline rush was incredible.

When we arrived at her friend's house, about four or five girls were waiting outside the building for us. They greeted me like an old friend, and I felt relieved. We all stood around talking and laughing for a long time. After the sun had set, two girls asked me if I wanted to listen to the latest music inside. Peanut encouraged me to check it out, so I did.

We took the elevator up at least 15 floors in the tall building and walked down long hallways to an apartment at the end. I went in with them, and we listened to all my '80s jams until I realized it had gotten super dark outside. I remember saying, "I'd better go meet back up with Peanut." We walked out to where we had been chilling earlier, but she was not there. I stood in the courtyard, looking to the left and the right for her, but she was nowhere in sight. As I looked at the two girls, they stared at me straight-faced without saying anything. Looking at them in confusion, I asked, "Where's Peanut?!"

They howled, slapped fives and yelled, "Yo, girl, she's gone! You're on your own!"

Before I could wrap my mind around what they had said, they turned and ran back into the building, slamming the door behind them. I immediately realized that I could not remember which apartment they had taken me to, didn't know how to return to the brownstone in Manhattan where I stayed with Arif and his family, and did not even know the address to ask someone to *help me* get there. I realized that I did not have the phone number to place a collect call at one of the telephone booths and that we had traveled there by train, and I did not even know which one to try to hop back. I felt trapped in a time warp. I feared throwing up or passing out on the sidewalk where the girls had deserted me, but I did neither. Instead, I did the only thing I could do. I started walking even though I had no idea where I was going.

As I walked, trying to put on a brave face, I saw a Hispanic man fighting a woman in the street without anyone stopping him. When I passed a police officer on a corner, I ducked my head, hoping he would not notice me. I desperately wanted to ask for help, but I dared not. I was afraid to admit that I was a runaway, unable to provide the address information for the place I had been staying at for the previous 10 months. So I kept walking without a clue as to where I was going, trying not to look like a terrified runaway. I had just been deserted by a demon named Peanut, who I'd thought finally wanted to be my friend. At that moment, I felt like an orphan with no hope and with no one to help me.

It felt like I walked all night, just stumbling along and trying not to cry from frustration and panic. Although I did not break down outwardly, something was brewing deep inside my soul with each tentative step I took. What springs to mind here is *"They wandered in the wilderness in a desolate way; they found no city to dwell in"* (Psalm 107:4–6). Just when I feared I would be lost forever, something quite unexplainable and mind-blowing happened. I felt like I had an out-of-body experience in which I was picked up from one place and put in another. The next moment, I walked up the steps to the Manhattan brownstone where the family lived and apprehensively knocked on the front door. My boyfriend snatched the door open and yelled in his thick New York accent, "Jackie, where have you been?! It's almost midnight!"

His stepdad, Robert, looked past me and up the block to the left. He inquired very angrily, "And WHERE is Peanut?!" My boyfriend pulled me into the apartment and wrapped his arm around me. The boiling hot volcanic pressure inside my soul erupted. I started screaming from a deeply wounded place, like someone in a horror movie: "She left me! Oh, *my Godddddddd*, she just left me!"

Simultaneously they practically yelled, "Left you where?!" I explained what had happened. Stunned, they asked, "But how did you get back here?!" I told them I had walked. Shaking heads and looking at each other with raised brows, they told me I could not possibly have done that. They knew all the natural odds stacked against me that would make walking alone from the Bronx to Manhattan impossible, especially at night. They repeatedly fired questions at me to get a different answer. Although I knew it did not make sense, I had no other explanation, and every word I said was true.

Suddenly, the front door flew open, and Peanut stepped inside. She looked at me as though I were a ghost, which confirmed that she had not expected to see me return. She saw me tearful and completely shaken to the core. Instead of apologizing or at least faking an apology for what she had done, she started laughing like a hyena. I would not have moved a muscle if Peanut had shown a half-ounce of remorse, but she hadn't. I saw red and charged at her like a bull charging at a matador in a Spanish bullring! It felt like she had been trying to get me killed out there on those New York streets, so I tried to kill her. For once, no one intervened to break up the fight, and I fought until I literally could not fight anymore. I am reminded now of how *"David and his men wept, until they had no more power to weep"* (1 Samuel 30:1–4).

After the fight with Peanut, I cried myself to sleep for several nights because I was physically and emotionally exhausted. The same week, I saw a news report saying an unidentified teenage girl had been found dead in the river with cinder blocks tied to her ankles. It occurred to me that I could easily have been found dead, and no one would have known what had happened to me.

About two weeks later, my boyfriend's mom asked him to go to the grocery store for her. Barely five minutes after he left, there was a soft knock at the front door, and his mom let a petite-framed white lady with a blond bob into the apartment. I immediately felt a sense of déjà vu as she entered the room and gingerly instructed me, "Jackie, please gather your things and come with me." Without looking at me, Ms. Sharon said, "I have heard that the police are searching for you down south, and I don't want to get arrested for harboring a minor." Perhaps thinking about what could have happened to me when her daughter abandoned me had sparked the liability light bulb in her mind.

After identifying herself, the woman revealed that she worked at Covenant House New York, which provided emergency shelter, food, and crisis care to homeless and runaway youth. I had no choice but to pack my meager belongings into black trash bags and leave the apartment with her. I didn't even get to say goodbye to Arif and never saw him again; his mom had wisely intercepted that. As we drove away, the lady told me she was taking me to a place called Spofford—Spofford Juvenile Detention Center. "Owned and operated by the New York City Department of Juvenile Justice (DJJ) for 54 years, Spofford was an intake facility for people under 15 years of age awaiting trial or placement in a larger facility.

Spofford is one of New York City's "secure detention" centers. In 1984, the Supreme Court described it as being "indistinguishable from a prison" in *Schall v. Martin*. The court would determine that the "pretrial detention of a juvenile pursuant . . . gives rise to injuries comparable to those associated with the imprisonment of an adult. In both situations, the detainee suffers stigmatization and severe limitation of his freedom of movement." The psychological toll of Spofford on its young detainees was especially evident in the 1980s when a record of 50 suicide attempts by teenagers was reported in a single year."[2]

Spofford was right back in the Bronx, where those hateful girls had deserted me just weeks before. We arrived at a vast, scary-looking place surrounded by barbed wire, just like an adult prison. Once inside, I was informed that I had to stay overnight until they found a more suitable place for me the following day. They placed me in the boys' unit because of limited space. The staff there strongly advised me that I was not to take my jacket off for any reason. My mind screamed, "Why not?!" But rather than asking the question, I kept my red and blue New York Giants starter jacket buttoned up to the neck.

Additionally, I slept on my stomach so no one would try to open it. Thankfully, I made it through the night unharmed. The following day, I was transported to a Long Island group home to await my court date. As I nervously sat in the cold courtroom three weeks later, a woman judge in an ominous black robe and rectangular glasses reviewed my case. She wordlessly placed it aside when she was finished. From behind the bench, she stared long and hard at me. There was a sense that she was trying to make up her mind about something.

Finally, the judge sighed loudly, and with her clasped hands positioned at her chin, she said, "Jackie, you've been here a long time, but you are an interstate runaway. New York is not a safe place, and you don't belong here. You've *got* to go home. If I put you on a plane back to North Carolina, do you promise not to get off the plane until it's time?" I had been gone for almost an entire year and realized I was now out of options, so I agreed to comply. Subsequently, I experienced my first plane ride as a 15-year-old runaway. It was a quick flight. When I arrived back in North Carolina, the Department of Social Services picked me up *at the plane gate* and placed me in foster care for six months. Mom and I entered counseling in preparation for my transition back home. The social workers hoped that things would be better and I wouldn't run away again.

Isn't it funny how our paths are intricately carved out before us? Years later, as a young adult, I obtained a criminal justice degree with an emphasis on juvenile delinquency. That allowed me to work with hundreds of teens in complex situations for two decades. I also gave financial support to Covenant House New York, the organization God sent to save me when I did not have the sense to save myself. I learned that He kept every covenant He made without failure.

I moved on with life and tucked those deserted days away, or so I thought. I learned firsthand that tucking experiences away was simply a quick fix, an effort at self-preservation that didn't mean the experience was gone or I was healed. This fact was proven to me when I was in my early 30s. I did something I'd wanted to do for a long time but hadn't been able to get any African American peers to buy into. The opportunity to go on a ski trip to a lodge in Virginia presented itself, and I was excited! My godsister, Tammie, introduced me to the group I was joining. She remembered I was interested in skiing, and I implicitly trusted her judgment regarding people connections. I went, and the fact that I was the only chocolate bunny in the group did not make me feel nervous. I loved winter, and the ski resort looked like what I had seen on television and read about in Danielle Steel's books.

I had purchased an all-day ski pass, which included a ski lesson at the top of the mountain, five levels up. As lesson time approached, we all piled into a lodge vehicle and headed up the mountainside. Each skier stepped onto a contraption similar to the airport walking escalators when it reached where they stood. The device circled the huge perimeter where many others were also taking lessons. Somehow, I was the last to make it back around the track. When I stepped off the track, I immediately searched for my group but couldn't find anyone.

I stood there in all my heavy ski gear, white Mary J. Blige-inspired sun blockers, and a trendy brown lumberjack hat with the fur trim snugly clasped under my chin. Anxiety began to spread rapidly throughout my body like spiderwebs. My mind screamed, "Where in the world is everybody?! Which way did they go?!" Despite looking all around for my group, I saw not one familiar face. As I stood in utter disbelief that everyone had vanished into thin air, a long-forgotten trigger squeezed my shoulder. I was suddenly catapulted backward in time. In a shocking flashback, I was 15 years old all over again.

Like it was yesterday, I was standing deserted in the Bronx courtyard without a way to connect with the one person who had brought me there. I began to have a panic attack, heavy breathing, a knotted stomach, and all. It felt like stars were circling my head. Even though I was standing still, I felt dizzy.

The Lord pulled me back to the present when I felt I would crumble to the ground on that ski slope. I took an intense breath, shook it off, and apprehensively went to seek assistance from the instructor. I explained the situation. After 20 minutes of searching and deliberation, he concluded the group must have gone back down the mountainside.

My mind began to race. Rage rose inside me like greenish-yellow bile, trying to expel itself from the body during sickness. I tried to control it but couldn't. My mind screamed, "Back down the mountain?! Without me?! How could they not notice that I was missing when I was the only chocolate thing in the whole group?! Why didn't they just wait for me?!"

The concerned instructor was kind enough to help me get back down the mountain to the entrance level. According to him, if I waited at the front, the group would eventually pass by. He was right. About an hour later, they showed up. They were laughing and just having a wonderful time. I, on the other hand, was simply livid by then. I was a Christian, but it took everything I had not to curse them out and start kung-fu fighting them as Carl Douglas had sung about back in the day!

Instead of going off, I listened to what they had to say but thought to myself they were without excuse. The members of that group all knew each other, and I was the visitor. My mind said, "You don't have to worry about me ever joining this group again!" My immature rage led me to believe *somebody* owed me something for my troubles. Deciding that I would get *something* positive out of that hellacious day, I went to the ticket purchase window and advised the management of the situation. They apologized for my miserable experience and made me feel better by refunding every cent of my money.

As I headed home, I forgave the group and pondered how another déjà vu experience had affected me so profoundly years later. I realized the enemy had used my childhood trauma and drama to send back a "defiling evil spirit" to see if I could still be moved by the threat of desertion (Matthew 12:44–45). Desertion is such an emotionally charged evil that some never recover from it. I am grateful that I faced my demons on that day, and although they attempted to shake me, they did not get the victory.

The enemy was slick and seized every opportunity to throw a brick through my windshield and deny me clear visibility. As the enemy threw an abandonment-laden brick at me, I responded wisely. Grace empowered me to pick that brick up and throw it right back, just like some characters do with live grenades in the movies.

*When
common sense failed,
God's covenant
prevailed.*

debilitated
verb
de·bil· i ·tat·ed

1. Showing impairment of energy
or strength; enfeeble
2. In a severely weakened state[1]

DEBILITATED: THE FIFTH DOCTOR

The day I first noticed prickly, tingling sensations in my fingertips and feet is forever etched in my mind. It felt like I had been playing in the snow although it was not snowing. I told my mom about the sensations, but she brushed them off as nothing to worry about.

I was 16 years old and in the 10th grade. My neighborhood was close to Rocky Mount Senior High, so I was accustomed to walking to and from school. I was not accustomed to my legs suddenly and completely giving out beneath me as I strutted up the front steps. Yep, one minute I was walking, and the next minute I was lying crumpled in a heap on the steps. I was taken home and began contending daily with a downward decline in my health. I had to stay home from school alone because Mama worked two jobs, and I understood she needed them to care for my younger siblings and me.

Derrick, a former boyfriend, heard through the grapevine that I was extremely sick and came to check on me. His hometown was Trenton, New Jersey, but he lived and went to school in Wilson, North Carolina. Derrick, whose nickname was Peanut—Lord have mercy, *another* Peanut—was a popular football player who was quite full of himself. Appearing to still care for me, Derrick drove back and forth to show support. He stayed out of school on some days to look after me while Mama was at work.

I'll never forget the day I was slowly inching to the bathroom to pee when, without warning, I began falling straight backward mid-step. It was like I was in slow motion, and I could not stop the fall. In distress, I weakly called Derrick's name. Just seconds before I hit the floor, he flew across the room and scooped me up like I was the football on the gridiron.

He held me close and said, "It's ok, baby, I've got you." He wiped my shameful, terrified tears and carried me to the commode where I had been heading. He placed me into position and assisted me without hesitation. I was so thankful that he had caught me and vowed never to forget it. Gratitude, however, can be a double-edged sword if we fail to understand that sometimes loyalty can be misplaced and needs an expiration date. I was late learning the lesson to *"not be entangled with a yoke of bondage"*

(Galatians 5:1). My mind believed I owed him more than I did, so this one act of heroism trauma-bonded us for over 10 years.

Unfortunately, my health got progressively worse instead of better. My Mom took me to four different doctors; however, no one could figure out what was wrong with me. Meanwhile, I became weaker and weaker every day. At this point, my walk was more like a vertical crawl. Every time I went to the doctor, they examined me from head to toe and took blood samples for lab work. Each visit ended with them sending me home without hope until my mom took me to the fifth doctor. I waited for what seemed like hours for the doctor to return after numerous tests. He read his clipboard notes and looked thoughtfully at me before finally speaking. He quietly asked me, "Jackie, what do you think is wrong with you?"

I swallowed hard to force down the colossal lump burning in my throat then tearfully replied, "Well—super long pause—I think I'm dying, and no one wants to tell me."

After months of my not knowing what was happening to me, there was an answer. This doctor diagnosed the situation, but it wasn't good. He said, "No, Jackie, you are not dying, but you are extremely sick. We need to counteract the great possibility of your major organs shutting down, and you must be hospitalized immediately so we can do that." He explained that the tests revealed I had contracted a rare illness known as Guillain-Barré Syndrome (GBS). I had never heard of it before.

In case you're curious, here are a few facts about GBS according to Mayo Clinic research:

> Guillain-Barré (gee-YAH-buh-RAY) syndrome is a rare disorder in which the immune system attacks the nerves. An acute bacterial or viral infection may trigger it. Weakness and tingling in your extremities are usually the first symptoms. These sensations can quickly spread, eventually paralyzing your whole body. Although most people recover from Guillain-Barré syndrome, the mortality rate is 4% to 7%. Between 60-80% of people regain walking ability at six months. Patients may experience lingering effects such as weakness, numbness, or fatigue. Paralysis can occur. Special blood treatments (plasma exchange and immunoglobulin therapy) can relieve symptoms, and physical therapy is needed. [2]

This debilitating illness had infiltrated my body like an invader from outer space without warning. It caused my immune system to turn on my nervous system, rendering me helpless. I did enter the ICU unit; however, contrary to the doctor's fears and mercifully, my major organs did not give out. However, GBS eventually shut my nervous system down, leaving my body 90% paralyzed. Lying flat on my back, I could only lift my forearms and turn my head from side to side as it rested on the pillow. I was unable to smile because my facial muscles had collapsed. It was hard for me to speak because I could barely open my jaws.

I thought the day I had a spinal tap in my lower back would be my last day on earth; such were the excruciating waves of pain that rolled through my entire body. According to the Mayo Clinic, "during a lumbar puncture, a needle is inserted between two lumbar bones (vertebrae) to remove a sample of cerebrospinal fluid. A lumbar puncture can help diagnose serious infections like meningitis and other central nervous system disorders, such as Guillain-Barre syndrome."[3]

The medical staff applied a local anesthetic to numb the pain during the lumbar procedure. I promise you it did not work. When I cried out upon the first insertion attempt, they stopped and repeated the numbing process, but I couldn't tell the difference. As they worked on my spine, I felt every bit of what I should not have been able to feel. While lying on my left side in the fetal position with nurses holding me in place, I cried a river of tears. When it was over, I continued to whimper as I was assisted back to my hospital bed from the procedure table. Although GBS attacked my physical body, *the Lord sustained me on my sickbed* (Psalm 41:3, NIV).

Previously, I had been the life of the party, jamming and giving dance lessons for $5 per person. And oh, my goodness, rap had been everything to me! Before I stepped up to the microphone, I would feel that "rap thing" fuel my heartbeat and put a thump in my soul. Creating bars, matching beats, and hearing excited crowds at community competitions were all part of what I had lived for as a teen.

It was horrifying to be unable to take care of myself. I could not chew, so of course, I could not eat. I could not brush my teeth. I could not bathe myself. I could not comb my hair. I could not even lift myself onto a bedpan when I had to use the bathroom. Nurses turned me over every two hours around the clock to prevent bedsores. My arms looked like a heroin addict's because I had so many IV needle marks. Because I have small veins, 50% of my inserts had to be attempted multiple times, further infuriating me. In my heart, I screamed, "I am just a 16-year-old girl! I don't understand why this is happening to me, and I hate it!" I hated all of it, but I could change none of it.

That mysterious illness attacked me in 1985. HIV and AIDS had hit the scene recently, and I was horrified to be informed during a hospital visit by a friend that people were saying I had it. While there, this person that I thought was my friend behaved as if she believed I had it. That perception had me cursing in my head; something gnarly may have leaked out. After she left, I cried my eyes out. I felt half-dead for a while, and I don't know if I was more hurt or angry.

To prevent another painful report from coming in unexpectedly, I decided I no longer wanted visitors. Then one day, a woman named Ms. Bertha T. Dempsey appeared out of nowhere. She was honey brown, spoke quietly, and wore glasses with classy outfits down to her stilettos. This woman didn't even know me; however, she began to visit me regularly when she heard about my illness at church. She read the Bible, prayed, and just talked to me. I was too angry to speak to her at first, but she returned every other day. As the months passed, we formed an amazing bond and grew to love each other a great deal. I am convinced she was an earthly angel, like Mary Poppins or Nanny McPhee, that God assigned to see me through that dark time.

A saying of unknown origins states, "Things often get worse before they get better." The seeds of kindness Ms. Dempsey sowed in me were preparing me for the darkest hour of my illness, which was still to come. One day as I lay paralyzed in that cold hospital bed, I overheard the nurses say from the hallway right outside my door that the doctors could do nothing more for me there. They must have thought I was asleep, but I was wide awake. Terror gripped my heart when I heard that the hospital was moving me to a rehabilitation center. Deep within, I knew just as surely as I knew my name that I would die if they sent me away, and I did not want to die.

I had been brought up in a Christian home and had been baptized, but I did not know Jesus in my heart. Even though I did not know Him, I began to cry and talk to Him on the inside because I still had trouble speaking aloud. Throughout the night, I lay on that bed crying and praying, "Jesus, *please* help me and save me from these people!" Exactly when the touch happened, I don't know. All I know is that I was sitting on the side of the bed when the morning nurse entered my room! Miraculously, my feet swung back and forth like sheer curtains blown softly by the wind. The nurse stopped, looked at me in amazement, and quickly backed out, yelling, "She's up! Oh, my God, she is UP!"

Other staff came rushing in to see what was happening and were astonished. From there, the slow healing process began. I started physical therapy to learn how to walk all over again. On day one, my assigned therapist, Joe, pushed my wheelchair to the end of the ramp. I had not seen myself since the day of my admission to the ICU. A skeleton stared back at me at the end of the ramp, and I cried in shock. With a kind squeeze on my shoulder, Joe encouraged me to stop crying and let him help me up from the chair so we could get started. I composed myself and then followed his strength training instructions.

Physical therapy was excruciating, but I did what I had to do a literal inch at a time. Although I eventually got much better, I was in a wheelchair when I finally left the hospital. I was still debilitated and unable to walk, but at that moment, it did not even matter. I had not been outside for what seemed like a year and felt like I was escaping from Alcatraz. In all that time, I had not smelled fresh air or felt unwanted raindrops pelt my skin during a storm. The sky was a sight I had only seen through my hospital window, and I had not felt the sun beaming down on my skin. I was beyond grateful to be done with those IV needle sticks so that my arms could stop looking like I was a heroin addict.

At home, I wheeled myself from room to room in that creaky wheelchair with the old gospel song, "Ask God in Faith," by Willis Pittman and the Burden Lifters, blasting on repeat. All I wanted was to walk again! I kept returning to physical therapy weekly, and after an incredibly long ordeal, I transitioned from a wheelchair to a walker. In the beginning, I had to walk slowly to regain my strength. A cane replaced my walker until the day came when I could walk without assistance. As I write this, my ears are filled with the sound of the wheelchair wheels turning. The sound touches my spirit and reminds me that God is a healer, especially for those who want to be healed (Luke 5:1–9).

Decades later, I remembered thinking that God had been trying to tell me something through that period of wheelchair-bound debilitation. Aha! Destiny was calling me as I wheeled myself around, but I did not perceive it. When I silently cried out for God while lying in that hospital bed, I had given my heart to Him. But I did not even realize it until I was mature enough to truly understand it. God was not surprised at my lack of comprehension and gave me the grace to continue growing and becoming. My ability to recognize the voice of God has evolved, and I have learned to recognize even the quietest whisper.

Loyalty
can sometimes
be misplaced & need
an expiration date.

destroyed
transitive verb
de·stroyed

1. to ruin the structure, organic existence, or
condition of also: to ruin as if by tearing to shreds
2 a: to put out of existence: KILL[1]

CHAPTER 4

DESTROYED: BLUE LIGHTS
FLASHING BEHIND ME

When you're 16 and find out you're pregnant, it's not fun. At least it was not for me. I was terrified because John and I had recently broken up, and when I told him about it, he emphatically denied the baby was his. Later he admitted to knowing it was his and offered to pay for an abortion, and I said no, which infuriated him. John screamed at me and insisted that he was going to Chowan College on a football scholarship and would not let anything stand in his way. He changed his stance about the pregnancy every week until I finally told him to just forget about it and go enjoy his football scholarship; I would not need him.

I kept my pregnancy secret, or so I thought. I discovered that John had told everyone who would listen that I was trying to trap him with a baby because he was a star athlete headed to college! I was afraid to tell my mama about the situation because I knew it would not go well. I thought I had it under control until things radically changed one morning at around 7:30 am. Mama had come home from her night job, and she kept quietly walking through my room which had Jack and Jill doors. The third time she walked through, I heard a voice say, "Get up right now, and go into the bathroom." I obeyed the voice and sat like a statue on the commode, pretending to relieve myself, but I was hiding. Time ticked by slowly as I sat there like a statue. Just when I thought it was safe to get up, the bathroom door swung open. Mama stood in the doorway, looking at me hatefully. I did not move or say anything, hoping she would leave. Instead, she said, "You think I don't know you're pregnant, but I do. What do you plan to do about doctor visits and caring for a baby?"

I was shaking and terrified to speak. It took me two whole minutes to find my voice. When I could speak, I said, "Well, I can walk down to the free health department near City Lake, and they will help me." She began screaming and talking incoherently. Trying not to make her angrier, I said, "Mama, you were 16 when you had me, so you should try to understand." Oh, Lord, why did I say that?!

She went off even more and screamed, "See, THAT'S your problem! You think you know everything and always love all the wrong people!"

The next thing I knew, she lunged at me. She had a brown nylon stocking stretched wide in her hands and tried to strangle me. I did not fight or even try to hit her. I just tried to get loose. She dropped the stocking in the struggle but put me in a headlock lighting fast and proceeded to bang my head against the side of the bathtub. I saw stars but kept struggling to get loose because I knew she was seriously trying to kill me. That single moment confirmed that there was no way she could love me, and it destroyed my love for her.

In desperation, I screamed for my brother Teddy's help. Since he always slept like a log and snored like a hog, he did not hear me. Miraculously, I got out of the headlock and tried to run through the bathroom door. Mama grabbed my baby blue cotton nightgown with white eyelet trim around the neckline and ripped it right down the front. I grabbed it and held it close to my body as I managed to escape the house. I took off running, hollering, screaming, and crying straight down the middle of West Thomas Street.

I was headed to my friend's house on North Howell Street when I heard loud sirens and saw blue lights flashing behind me. As the police approached, I stopped running. They thought I had just been raped. I hysterically related what had happened as they placed me in the car. They took me to my friend's house around the corner and told me to wait while they went to my house to investigate my story.

The police returned and informed me that Mama had a different story that twisted things around to make me the perpetrator. She said I had tried to strangle *her* while she sat asleep in her favorite chestnut brown armchair. My mind raged at what I heard because I had not done and would never think of doing, let alone trying, something like that. Mama never apologized for the unhinged, angry act she committed against me that could have killed me. It destroyed any flickering hope I had that maybe, just maybe, she hadn't meant to hurt me.

The investigation of our home confirmed signs of a bathroom struggle. Pieces of my blue nightgown were on the floor, corroborating my side of the story. The police stated that the chair Mama had claimed to be asleep in was flush against the wall. According to them, the chair's placement left no room for me to try to strangle her from behind as she had claimed. Mama also did not have any marks on her neck. The police said they believed me based on their observations, yet it was my word against hers. They asked if I could remain at my friend's house until things cooled down, and her mom said I could.

I remained with them for four weeks until my Aunt Joann, who lived in Virginia, heard about the situation from my Aunt Lois. Because they both believed in me, they devised a plan for Aunt Joann to pick me up. She took me home with her and provided for my daily needs. She had three children and a boyfriend living with her. The children were no problem, but I could not get along with her man. He was unnecessarily mean to the children. I could not stand seeing or hearing it. He said I was too mouthy when I told him he needed to leave those children alone. They were terrified of him, and something inside me compelled me to speak out in their defense. My standing up for the kids brought about constant conflict. Aunt Joann wanted to keep the peace in her home, so I could not stay there much longer. She had tried, but I was back in Rocky Mount at my friend's home within six months. While they were good people, different variables prevented me from remaining there for a long time. Plus, I was also eight-and-a-half months pregnant by then. I genuinely did not know what to do or where to go.

Do not ask me how he found out where I was, but my ex-boyfriend, the New Jersey jock, just showed up at Linda's front door unexpectedly. I told him what had happened with Mama and how afraid I was to return there. He said he understood what I was saying, but my mama must have just been in a hurt, blind rage when she attacked me. He said he didn't think she was still angry with me, so I should be ok. Derrick said I needed to be in more conducive living conditions and get help caring for the baby. I listened to him. By the end of the day, he had convinced me that I needed to go back and see how things turned out.

As Derrick drove me to Mama's new home in the country, I reflected on the terrifying struggle for my life in that tiny bathroom. Deep down inside, I knew that the episode was more than Mama's simply being angry with me, and I knew it was more than just hurt. Years passed before more information and revelations emerged about the generational curses and mental illness railway tracks that ran through my family.

As I tearfully thought over my present dilemma, reality hit me. I was now 17 years old and desperately needed help. Mama's actions had destroyed every ounce of love and trust I had for her, but what else could I do? As much as I feared dealing with my mother, I was more scared of caring improperly for the baby.

Realizing I had to take my chances for the baby's sake, I went home, but I was a nervous wreck, not knowing if the bathroom episode would be repeated. I was panic-stricken at the thought that I might not be able to escape again. I simply could not stay there with her, so I came up with a plan. In two months, I earned my GED from Edgecombe Community College, found a job at Texfi Blends, and rented an apartment on Arlington Street. Within a few months, I left my mama's home, looking for peace, and I thought I'd found it too, only to learn that it would not last. This proud obtainment would soon also be destroyed.

*God is
bigger than
generational curses
and mental illness.*

devastated
adjective
dev·as·tat·ed

1: brought to a state of ruin or destruction
2: emotionally shattered or distraught[1]

CHAPTER 5

DEVASTATED: "SOMEONE HAS HURT YOUR BABY"

My beautifully gifted and incredibly loved 10-month-old son had not been feeling well. He was being treated at home for a nasty cold that needed to run its cycle. Three hours before I was scheduled to go to my second-shift job at Texfi Blends, the babysitter called to say she was sick. Bummer! I had to get to work at 4 pm! I contacted two people to see if they could help; however, no one was available on such short notice. I was about to notify my job that I could not make it in; however, my boyfriend Kenny said he would keep Jawaan for me. Cool! Kenny had been in our lives since Jawaan had been a few months old, and the family thought highly of him. He had kept Jawaan once or twice before and taken him on park outings, so I was comfortable with the plan.

I called home at lunchtime and received the update that Jawaan's cold was the same. He had just received a cough medicine dose and finally settled down. As soon as I got off at midnight, I went straight home to my apartment on Arlington Street in Rocky Mount, of which I was so proud. Entering the bedroom, I flicked the bright ceiling lights on and sang, "Hi, *Jawaannnnnn*," thinking it would wake him up as usual. Hopefully, he was feeling better. I walked over to his crib, pulled the soft covers back, and tickled him while continuing to sing out his name. He didn't wake up or move. I repeated my actions. Still no response. He was limp like a rag doll when I picked him up. I began to panic, thinking that his temperature must have gotten too high while he was sleeping and somehow affected him. Oh my Lord!

I did not call the ambulance. Mama worked a private duty nursing assignment just around the corner. My only thought was that she would know what was wrong and what needed to be done. With the baby wrapped tightly in my arms, I rushed out of the apartment. Kenny came out right behind me and jumped in the driver's seat while I held my son. Like a madwoman, I banged on the residence door where Mama worked until she opened it. As I thrust the baby into her arms, I said, "Mama, Jawaan is sick, and I don't know what's wrong!"

She looked at the baby and answered, "Stay here with my patient; I'm taking him to the hospital." She never considered the potential consequences of leaving her patient unattended. God's mercy kept her from getting into trouble that night.

Time seemed to stand still as I waited for Mama to call me. She never did. The ER doctor called me directly and said, "Jackie, listen closely to me. Someone has hurt your baby. He is in a coma and bleeding on the inside. He needs emergency surgery to relieve pressure on his brain caused by swelling. You need to get here right now."

Kenny was there with me and asked what was going on as I hung up. Then, in shock and devastation, I simply told Kenny, "I have to get to the hospital right now."

He jumped up and said, "Get in the car then, and let's go!" He threw the hazard lights on and drove me to the emergency room entrance at about 100 mph.

During the drive to Nash General Hospital, I tried to think of what in the world could have happened to my baby. It never occurred to me to associate the doctor's "Someone has hurt your baby" report with Kenny. Kenny pulled up at the emergency room entrance. I jumped out and ran inside, looking for my child and the doctor who had called me, while Kenny parked the car.

As soon as I walked in, I felt like I was in a sci-fi movie. The police were already there and pulled me aside for questioning before even allowing me to see my baby. I told them where I had been from 4 pm to midnight and that Kenny had looked after the baby for me.

The police asked me, "Ok, *where* is Kenny now?" I told them he was parking the car. Without another word, the police went outside and arrested him on the spot for suspicion of felony child abuse. *Kenny?! No way!* It still never once occurred to me that Kenny had harmed my child. When the child's father had acted as if the child didn't exist, that young man had stepped in and helped me in every way he could. He loved that child, and that child loved him. I could not understand how Kenny could have done what they said he did.

Devastated does not convey how I felt when they finally took me to see my son, Jawaan. Standing beside that hospital bed, I died 1,000 times as I tried to see his little body through the tubes flowing everywhere. It was undoubtedly the most appalling, heartbreaking thing I had ever seen with my own eyes. There are no words to describe the devastation of that moment and I would have immediately swapped places with Jawaan.

It took the detectives a solid week to determine how such an inconceivable crime could have occurred. At first, Kenny said nothing out of the ordinary had happened the entire day or night. Then he said that Jawaan kept crying, and as he walked and rocked him, he accidentally hit the baby's head on the door frame.

Next, Kenny stated that Jawaan's temperature had gotten incredibly elevated and he had needed to be cooled down. Kenny explained that he had gotten into the shower with the baby and fallen on the slippery floor.

Finally, Kenny told another tale that was determined to be the truth, at least the natural portion of it. Kenny said that my baby had been asleep in his crib and that he had checked on him regularly throughout the evening. He then said that a voice had woken him up during the night and told him to get the baby out of the crib, so he had done that. Kenny informed the police that the voice had told him to take the baby back to bed and sit at the foot of the bed. According to him, the voice had subsequently told him to lift the baby and throw him across the room into the wall. So he had done that. The young man reported hearing two thuds that the detectives surmised occurred when the baby first slammed into the wall and then when he hit the floor. Lastly, Kenny said he was instructed to pick the baby up, place him back in the crib, cover him with the blanket, and return to bed.

While Kenny was in jail awaiting trial, two things caused me to unravel further. First, Derrick came to see me again with a proposal to bail Kenny out of jail and "wrap that situation up." As devastated as I was, I had the common sense to know what he meant and said, "Absolutely NOT! I do not want ANY part of something like that, and I mean it! Please promise to let the police handle it." Fortunately, he agreed, but he asked me to notify him immediately if I changed my mind. Second,

Kenny wrote me a letter, emphatically stating that he did not understand what had happened since he loved my son and would never hurt him. When the detectives told him he had committed this monstrous act, he had asked for forgiveness and expressed his wish to die. He was tested for drugs, and the results were negative because he did not do drugs. Psychological testing ruled out insanity. As it turned out, he unsuccessfully tried to commit suicide inside the cell.

While he was locked up, my child remained in a coma. Because of the extent of the injuries, the doctors warned me that he might never wake up. They said that if he did wake up, he would probably be a vegetable and need to be institutionalized. I sat alone outside the door to his room on a bench, beyond devastated. I began to cry, thinking to myself, "Oh my God! I am 18 years old. My baby is only 10 months old and dying. I don't know what to do." I didn't know Jesus, but I prayed to Him that night. I knew how to pray because I had been raised in the church all my life. I prayed, "Lord, you heard what those doctors said, but I don't want to lose my baby; I need my baby. Please, Lord, help my baby live, and I will do the best I can with him. I just want him to live no matter what."

It seemed as if the coma would never end. I will never forget the night that my adult cousin, Mary Helen, encouraged me to go home to shower and try to sleep. She said she would stay the night. For the first time, I went home as suggested. When

I finally fell asleep, the phone rang. I jumped up, knowing deep in my heart that it was the hospital. Indeed, it was, and they advised me to get there immediately because my baby had already stopped breathing twice. I flew to the hospital as fast as possible, praying the whole way. I was devastated at the thought of finding my baby dead when I arrived, but he was not. Praise God my child was still alive!

More weeks passed, and finally, OH HAPPY DAY, God had heard my prayers and answered them. Jawaan opened those brown eyes! He woke up, but he needed a lot of help. Before the horrific events, my "hyperactive from birth" bundle of joy had just begun walking. Now he had to learn how to do everything from scratch. When the doctors had done all they could, they decided to send him home. They informed me that I would need to suction out his tracheotomy three times daily before he could be discharged. *What?!* I told them, "No way; I will pass slam out trying to do something like that!" They insisted there were no other options, so I trained on caring for the trach daily. The procedure was nasty, and the stench took my breath away, but I did it *without* passing out or throwing up! Thankfully, Mama let us move in with her again. To God be the glory, she helped us get through that long, arduous journey to recovery for almost a year.

The Holy Spirit told me years later, while I was studying at Virginia Union Christian University, that Satan had entered

Kenny's subconscious sleep state. *But how, God? How?* The Holy Spirit showed me a snapshot of about 10 African masks I had purchased at a yard sale hanging on the walls throughout the apartment. Maturity in Christianity helped me understand that demonic spirits need a place to live, and they looked for a place where they could hide until they found an opportunity to come out and do their evil works. Who knows how long they had lain dormant in those masks? Those mind-controlling spirits that came out of hiding, overtook Kenny, and used him as a puppet because he was susceptible devastated our lives. But God!

I say, "But God!" because God divinely intervened. Not only did Jawaan live, but he is far from the gravely predicted vegetable requiring institutionalization. Praise Jehovah God Almighty! If you were to meet my 35-year-old son today, you would love him! Unless I told you, you would never know what he went through in his first year of life. Jawaan does have some special needs; however, he is extremely high-functioning. He was always at the head of his Compensatory Education class at Nash Community College and his group home. He has a joyful and helping spirit with the gift of encouragement.

Throughout the years, people of all genders and ethnicities have said that makes him most memorable and causes him to stand out above other young folks. That wonderful spirit has granted him incredible favor throughout his life in countless ways. God turned what was meant to be lifelong devastation into blessed preservation!

Demonic spirits
look for a
susceptible
place to live.

demoralized
verb
de·mor·al·ized

2 a: to weaken the morale of:
DISCOURAGE, DISPIRIT
b: to upset or destroy the normal
functioning of c: to throw into disorder[1]

CHAPTER 6

DEMORALIZED: SLOWLY SLIPPING AWAY

He held a 15-inch knife blade against my neck. With a hateful, drunk-as-a-skunk voice, my husband rasped, "Move one inch, and I will cut your whole blankety-blanking head completely off!"

I believed him. Afraid to even breathe, I did not move. All I could do was cry inside and pray, "Jesus, please help me." He released my neck but threw me to the floor like a sack of potatoes. I thought he was done, but he was far from it. Before I could get back on my feet, he jumped on top of me like a sleek black panther. His professionally licensed boxer fists rained blow after blow down onto me. He began choking me, stopping the blood flow to my brain. I cried more desperately inside, "Jesus, PLEASE help me!" Unable to speak because of the pressure against my throat, I heard my voice saying, "My babies will not have a mother." Miraculously, my husband listened to what was really God's whisper through his rage. He instantly released me and, without looking back, walked away.

As was typical of intimate partner violence, the apologies came with a few days of good behavior. I just kept going day by day. My main concern was making sure the children were okay. Battered wife syndrome was my reality: My periodic decision to leave was snuffed out whenever I thought about the possibility of his changing. The experience of growing up without a father and its impact on me overrode my desire to leave. Foolish pride and a dumb dream kept me shackled to insanity.

I tried separation, but it never lasted. Hearing the children crying for Daddy for hours was unbearable, and I could not mentally and emotionally take it. Seeing their disappointment, I kept trying to work on the marriage, hoping things would improve, but it was a constant emotional rollercoaster ride. In typical roller-coaster fashion, domestic violence creeps deliberately up the tracks: clickety-clack, clickety-clack. It causes the same sinking feeling as the roller coaster when it rises slowly and experiences a free fall. As a kid, I was always terrified of roller coasters, screaming for Jesus and feeling sick to my stomach for hours afterward. That was what being battered was like. Sometimes, there was no warning. Mondays through Thursdays were better than Fridays through Sundays, though.

I will never forget the Friday night when I slid to the bottom left-hand corner of the pit. Around midnight, I was sound asleep in our black lacquer queen-sized bed. Despite being a light sleeper, I was completely caught off guard. Suddenly, my husband's hand forcefully flung the covers off me from out of nowhere. I heard loud cursing as he literally snatched me out of bed and immediately put me in a chokehold. He yelled, "Where in the hell have you been?!"

Trembling in terror, I tried to say, "Nowhere. I've been right here; home all night." He vehemently insisted I was lying, and so it began. Again, I prayed, "Jesus help me." I tried to calm John down so that the mess would not wake the children, who were sleeping in their rooms just up the hallway. It didn't work. An enraged person cannot be reasoned with, as I have learned from experience.

Those demons inside him, controlling him, saw me trying to remain calm. They went off even more. He viciously beat me like I was one of his opponents of equal height and weight in the boxing ring. *Oh my God!* I could not be quiet anymore. Pain and terror boiled up like a volcano and spilled over. Against my will, I began to scream at the top of my voice for him to stop. I cried over and over that I had not been out with anyone. I broke free from his iron-fist hold and ran towards the front door as fast as possible. I almost made it too. One more step would have done it. However, it did not happen that way because that six-foot, three-inch frame was much faster than my five-foot frame.

As I made that last step toward safety, he reached out and caught me with one hand. That one enraged hand ripped the baby blue linen nightgown I was wearing straight down the middle and right from my body. My goodness, baby blue cotton nightgowns were bad karma for me back then! The next thing I knew, another blow knocked me through the storm door, and I landed flat on my back in the front yard. Since I had been asleep in bed with nothing underneath, my whole body was completely exposed.

The pouring rain pelted down and immediately soaked me, shifting my state of shock at what had just happened. I tried to move, but it was impossible. It felt like an Amtrak train had run over me, backed up, and ran over me again. I was stunned and barely conscious. Unable to rise, I was like the woman who *"could in no way raise herself up"* (Luke 13:11).

I lay there, crying and screaming, screaming and crying, like a wounded animal out in the woods, all alone and caught in a hunter's trap. Broken and battered, I just wanted to disappear: pouf! At that moment, I did not care whether I lived or died. I preferred the latter. As I lay there, my mind was slowly slipping away. My experience proved the saying, "There's a thin line between sanity and insanity." I felt movement just before the last piece of my mind fell over the edge of the ledge. Soft yet strong arms picked my naked, bruised body up from the muddy ground. Through swollen eyes, in the dark of the night, I saw with intensified shame that it was my male neighbor. I did not even know his name, but he had come to my rescue. He carried me into his apartment, laid me, dripping wet, on a leather couch, and covered me with a warm blanket. The Holy Spirit carefully loved and provided shelter for me through the kindness of a stranger. It was an enactment of Ezekiel 16:6, which declares, *"And when I passed by you and saw you struggling in your own blood, I said to you in your blood, 'Live!' Yes, I said to you in your blood, 'Live!'"*

Disguised as my neighbor, that angel asked me if I wanted to call someone to help me. I called Tammie, my godsister. James, her then husband, answered the phone and reminded me she was out of town. Despite my attempts to mask it, his police detective eardrum heard the trauma in my voice, and he demanded to know what had happened. Even though I was ashamed, I told him what had happened minus the fact that my husband's abuse had almost snatched away my sanity.

He spoke with authority: "Sis, tell me where you are; I'm coming." Lightning fast, James arrived in his rimmed-out, burnt orange two-door Toyota Supra with a gray sweatsuit and Adidas sneakers in hand. On that traumatic night, the Holy Spirit moved two compassionate men to stop what they were doing and respond to destiny's call to come and rescue me. Such grace.

In times past, I had called the police multiple times when the kids' dad had beaten me but dropped the charges before the court date. Not this time. John had thoroughly beaten out my deep-seated belief that the children needed their daddy. This recent calamity shut down my fear of being alone and starting over with someone new one day. Without a single doubt, I knew I would *never* survive another night like that Friday night. I did not withdraw the formal complaint before the court date. Unfortunately, though, I left the court feeling demoralized again. The judge and the district attorney, both males, made me feel as though I must have done *something* to warrant the treatment I described *or* I was flat-out lying. After all the courage it had taken me to finally face this domestic violence demon, I could not believe what I was hearing.

As I stood there, trying to be brave and not run out of that courtroom screaming and crying in utter humiliation, I gained clarity on why so many women who suffered domestic violence did not contact the authorities. It was because they knew they wouldn't receive justice. I vowed never to return to a courtroom again for a domestic violence act committed against me. The one saving grace that resulted from that fiasco was that my children's father saw that I was DONE with being beaten, and he never laid another hand on me. There was no more physical abuse, but many other freight trains kept coming down the tracks—clickety-clack. Some I may never voice aloud.

Where had the time gone? Suddenly, I was 29 years old. It was August 1999, and we would cross into a new decade in less than four months. The entire world was super hyped about the new millennium. Not me. It sickened me to realize that I would have been doing this, living in this hellacious relationship for a whole decade. In eight months, I would be 30 years old. I only felt pure desperation as I thought, "This can't be the life God has for me. There must be more or life just ain't worth it."

Finding myself at a crossroads that Saturday afternoon, I fell on the living room floor. They say that "big girls don't cry." Hmph! They'd better ask someone who will be REAL! I cried a river of tears on that floor, not because I wanted to but because the levee broke. They say, "Cover girls don't cry after their faces are made." I cried every carefully applied stroke of makeup completely off. My face looked like an abstract painting where the artist had slung the brush and let the colors land where they may. The tears flowed for hours.

What in the world made me cry so much? I cried because I knew I was too bright for this bull jive. I cried because I didn't understand why I had ever gotten back with his good-looking but good-for-nothing self in the first place. I cried because I instantly realized the main reason I had done so was that I had promised *never* to be like Mama and have different baby daddies for my children. I cried harder as I realized exactly how judgmental I had been of my mama regarding that.

I cried because I remembered how, years before, I had cried for seven days straight before the wedding, wanting to call it off, but I had been unable to. I cried because, foolishly, I had been more concerned about what people would have thought and said if I had done so. I cried as I recalled a counseling session with a devout church mother towards the end of my first year of marriage. I had shamefully confided in her about my being a battered woman with two children and not knowing what to do. I cried extra hard as I recalled her response. Her voice had been confident and faith-filled, so I had placed every ounce of my new Christian hope on her. Without hesitation and with complete conviction, that church mother had looked me in the face while softly patting my hand and had said, "Stay. Every Christian has a cross to bear, and this one must be yours. Just keep praying and believing. Jesus will help you."

I was confused and did not know how to respond, so I nodded in silent acquiescence. I was trying to learn the Bible and live right. While studying and trying to memorize the scriptures, I learned that Christians sometimes went through many hurtful things for the glory of God. I decided to obey what I believed was God speaking through the mouth of His servant. Having admired the church mother's anointing, I trusted her to guide me to the right answer. Her misguided ignorance and mishandling of the word of God helped lead me to what seemed like a lifetime more of a hellacious existence. It was years before I broke free from improper discernment of the difference between a cross for the glory of God and an albatross that caused the heart of God to grieve.

Looking back on that encounter much later, I realized something. The church mother, regarded as a highly esteemed, well-seasoned woman of God, had shown no prayerful concern for a young, battered woman. She had not taught me in a way that promoted life (Titus 2:3–5). I wonder what would have happened if she had instead said, "Sister Jackie, Jesus died so that we can live the best life possible. Being beaten IS NOT a good way of life for anyone, no ma'am, no way, no how! God is interested in your safety and preserving your life" (John 10:10).

Domestic violence was an evil that completely warped my natural mind. In retrospect, I wonder if the reasoning behind the Church Mother's answer was that it was the advice she had at some point received herself. The answer is none of my business. I can't say with 100% certainty that a different response would have caused me to get off the battered woman syndrome train that was bound to end in destruction. But I wonder about this sometimes: Suppose she had *tried* to give me a different answer, a spirit-inspired response; how different might my path have been?

Suddenly, I saw a clip from *American Gangster* about Frank Lucas's life flash in front of me. In one scene, all the family members involved in Frank's drug business got locked up by the Feds in a massive sting. His mom, played by the actress Ruby Dee, was beside herself and slapped the taste out of his mouth when he did not take responsibility for the arrests. Frank's Mom said, "If you had been a preacher, your brothers would have been preachers; if you had been a soldier, they all would have been soldiers. You know, they all came here because of you. You called, and they came running. That is because they look up to you. They always expect you to know what's best."

That was my state of mind when I went to visit the church mother. But like I said, I am honestly not sure I would have left if she had advised me to. Where responsibility and accountability are concerned, two points stand out to me: The first is "Shame on John for the first time he allowed himself to abuse me." The second is "Shame on ME for every time after that because the first time should have been the last time."

I knew I had failed to love myself, but I didn't know what loving myself looked like or understand how to do it. I forgave myself for what I didn't know, but on my knees, I continued crying. I cried most of all when I realized that although I had initially tried to protect my pride, I had not a shred of pride left. It had been beaten out of me long ago. I cried because I suddenly realized John wasn't fit to touch, let alone tie, the shoes on my feet! I cried because the day of complete reckoning had arrived. Destiny was calling my name from beneath the train wreck's ashes. I had to answer. I had to take responsibility for allowing myself to be demoralized and treated like dirt beneath his feet. I cried and I cried and I cried because I had been lost in gross darkness for a very long time. Lucidity was taking its rightful place, and I was unwilling to endure another year of oxygen deprivation. I knew I had to do something I had never done before, so I decided to put out a fleece before the Lord because I was desperate.

I will never forget the prayer I prayed through my tears:

> Lord, I have tried everything I know, and each year is worse than the year before. I am so confused about my Christian duty, my life, the lives of my children, and their needs. I don't want to do this anymore. I want to be free, but I will stay if it is Your will for me to stay. If my leaving is okay with You and You will help me, please speak to me by the end of this year. Please allow me to hear Your voice before the new millennium begins so that I will know what to do. Lord, talk to me crystal clear so I can comprehend it more than my messed-up emotions. Let me be sure that it was YOU who said it. And Lord, even if I don't like it, I will accept Your will if I'm sure it's You. In the name of Jesus, Amen.

I thought I'd get an answer by the end of the year, perhaps in December. Nope. I said that prayer in July, and in less than a month, I received what I immediately recognized as God's answer in such a traumatic way that nothing in me thought I would survive it. What was God's response? My mother knocked at the front door of my home at around 11 pm. She stood at the door looking very troubled. She asked my then husband, "Son, have you been home all night?" He looked back at her but said nothing. She asked again, more emphatically, "*Sonnnnn*, have you been home all night?" Again, silence.

Looking from one to the other like a tennis match spectator, I spoke up and said, "No, Mama, he just got in a little while ago. Why? What is going on?!"

She responded, "The police are at Teddy's house with Gal. She said John was there tonight and raped her."

Everything started spinning as the syllables tumbled out of Mama's mouth. That Amtrak traveling at 150 mph hit my family circle head-on. Gal was the wife of my brother, Teddy, and one of my closest friends. We all spent lots of time together; our children were around the same ages and best buddies. My mama was Mama and Grandma to all of us, and our combined family gatherings were a considerable part of her life. A reported rape was unthinkable, yet the bearer of shocking news stood here at the front door demanding an answer, praying to hear somebody say it wasn't so.

A sudden thought came to me that made my blood run cold. Jesus! This man who'd said he was just going to the corner store had been away for over four hours. While the children's dad was out, I had been sitting in bed, studying the tragedy of Tamar and Amnon (2 Samuel 13). It was the heartbreaking account of a brother who became insanely obsessed with and raped his beautiful half-sister, King David's daughter.

I remember combing through that chapter repeatedly and thinking, "With all the available women in the world, why would he do this to his sister? Why would he bring shame and pain to his family like that?" I could not begin to fathom the demoralization Tamar had experienced. It wouldn't have ended that night but would have kept going due to the customs of the time.

Oh my GOD! This hellacious news in the form of a mind-boggling question was it. It was the answer. I knew that this was God's answer to my prayer and that I was not to stay. Did I rejoice at the answer? No! I cursed like a madwoman into the night sky. I ranted and raged at God as I repeatedly shouted that I could not believe He would allow such a tragedy to happen. Quietly, He said, "You asked Me to speak, and I have spoken."

Blubbering and stuttering in disbelief, I raged back, "But that's not fair! You know You did NOT have to let this mess happen! I was about to leave five years ago! I had finally found the courage to file the divorce, and then YOU had Mother Augst prophesy to me in that doggone prayer room!" Mocking her voice, I verbalized to God what that godly prayer warrior who knew nothing about my situation had said: "Baby, God says to go back. Go back, go back, go back. Go back, and He will bless you."

I knew those words pertained to the fact that I had silently filed for divorce the week before. I also knew there was no chance in HELL that I would go back! It had taken everything to get where I should have been long before then. Before she uttered the second "go back," I was shaking my head to emphatically indicate, "No." It felt like hours passed as I screamed and hollered on the prayer room floor. I drove home, still crying. I intended to act like that noontime visit had never even happened. My spirit had other plans.

That fierce little woman who shook her Bible in the air as she spoke with unwavering conviction would not go away. The unique quality of Mother Augst's voice—squeaky yet powerfully arresting—was so compelling that it sounded like it had to be part of the great cloud of witnesses. I couldn't escape it. I could not sleep, eat, or rest. There was a physical churning in the pit of my stomach that I just knew was not like the situation with the church mother. It lasted for about three days, and I knew this was the Holy Spirit.

The moment I told God, "Yes," the churning stopped. And you know what? I did see the hand of God move in the marriage. Initially, John began attending church and even joined the men's choir. He was coming home much better and putting forth a noticeable effort there, but none of it was consistent over the long term. The train ride was excruciatingly long, with no clear destination or estimated arrival time.

The intensity of the memory had overtaken me for a moment. I snapped back to the present. Wiping uncontrollable tears, I vehemently said, "God, just look at what this has done to me. Just *lookkkk* at what it has done to our families! Why this?! Why her?! You could have just spoken! You could have just told me Your answer, talked back to me like I had talked to you! You did NOT have to let all this mess happen, and You know it!"

As my crying subsided, God softly said,

> Jackie, you wouldn't have heard me. Remember your prayer to Me on the living room floor? You said, "Please allow me to hear Your voice before the new millennium begins so that I will know what to do. Lord, talk to me crystal clear so I can comprehend it more than my messed-up emotions. Let me be sure that it was YOU who said it. And Lord, even if I don't like it, I will accept your will if I'm sure it's You. In the name of Jesus, Amen."

What?! Though gentle, God's reminder of my request assaulted all five of my senses. Looking up to heaven, I ranted, "Are You KIDDING me?!" Yes, those were my words verbatim, but I was one black woman, mad at God. I screamed and wailed in agony, "Okay, God, okay, but what is the *PURPOSE* of this unnecessary pain, Lord?!" With hands raised in disbelief, I heatedly repeated, "Exactly *WHAT* is the purpose?!"

God calmly but unapologetically responded, "Daughter, it was so severe because I *severed it* in the heavens." I heard that with my mind and spirit over my heart and soul. Despite all I felt, I suddenly understood that my entire moral system had to be utterly offended to disentangle me from that marriage. That Amtrak train crash was a godsend that finally set me free.

I was still mad as you-know-what; nonetheless, I remembered to ask one more thing: "Ok, Lord, what about the prophetic promise I did not ask for in the prayer room? What in the world was that all about?!"

God compassionately honored me with an answer. The Holy Spirit let me know that although God had a sovereign will, He had granted His children permissive will. I was advised that there had been a window of time when God's will would have happened if my children's father had participated with the Holy Spirit. God would not override John's permissive will to continue doing what felt good to him. Lordy, talk about being careful what you ask for! I resolved never to question the situation again. My children and I would move on.

Three short weeks later, before I could catch my breath from that train wreck, the flood of the century, Hurricane Floyd, ripped through our region, leaving massive destruction in its wake. I was still reeling from the calamity inside my home, but God kept my children and me safe from further harm. As we were evacuated from our home by boat in the predawn hours,

I felt like I was being broken apart, but God did not let it go down that way. He graciously provided refuge in a local church. We waited there, huddled in the darkness with other hopeful neighbors until it was safe to return home to survey the storm's aftermath.

Upon my return home, I saw damage all up and down our street. *Oh my God!* Right next door to me, the floodwaters had risen to the very top of the front door; our neighbors had already put large, soaked items on the curb to be discarded. The water had gone no further than our second doorstep. As I entered my perfectly dry front door, I knew we were highly blessed. And whether I liked God's methodologies or not, I had survived both calamities. Jesus kept us through it all, and I was free *before* the millennium came in, just as I had requested.

*A moment of
lucidity
replaced
oxygen deprivation!*

deployed
verb
de·ployed

2: to spread out, utilize, or arrange
for a deliberate purpose[1]

CHAPTER 7

DEPLOYED: PRISON REVEALED MY PURPOSE

You'll foolishly ride in the devil's car when you don't know who you are or that you're predestined for greatness. Indeed, I rode in it and enjoyed every minute until the day I was rendered speechless. My boyfriend, Derrick, who I thought was madly in love with me, pulled the car to the curb in front of someone's home. He reached across me as I sat there in the front passenger seat. I thought he was going for something beneath the leather seat on the floorboard. To my jaw-dropping disbelief, his hand went into MY **** pocketbook and came out with a quart-sized Ziploc bag filled with cocaine. *Oh my God!*

Suddenly, I saw myself behind steel bars, staring out for the rest of my natural life. If we had been stopped, I would have been unable to explain that the drugs were not mine. I almost had a Fred Sanford "I'm coming, Elizabeth!" moment when I realized that this young man, whom I said I was in love with, was about to get me *life* in federal prison. I had never smoked a cigarette or marijuana. While I had tasted Budweiser beer, I had never drunk a whole can. Other than on TV and in movies, I had never even seen cocaine.

While I had never seen it, ignorance is without excuse. At 16, I did not know that my 18-year-old boyfriend, whom I had innocently met at the Sports World Skating Rink, sold drugs. He lived out of town and usually visited me on weekends because we were in school. He told me he had gotten his car and fly gear from his dad, a successful business owner. Suddenly, I saw what had been hidden from me all along.

I was livid and could not recall precisely when he seized the opportunity to place that bag in my possession. I demanded to be taken home that instant and told him I was done with his black ***! Even though I stopped seeing him, I still cared for him. How he could have used me like that, and the thought of what could have happened to me was sickening. The situation hurt terribly, but thank God we were not stopped by the police on that day. I had escaped that trick bag and was spared from having to replace my full name with a series of numbers.

Funny how these things have a way of carving out an unimagined path. As a correctional officer at Fountain Correctional Center for Women, I rediscovered the buried memory of unknowingly having a quart-sized bag of cocaine planted on me. It allowed me to have great compassion when on occasion, I met an inmate who shared a similar story of ignorance, oblivion, and plain old stupidity. In retrospect, I had to own that, from time to time, some things had raised questions that I had explained away. I had to take responsibility for riding with the devil back then. My message to the women at the correctional center was that they, too, had to take some responsibility for their actions.

Despite multiple chances to be sucked into sin through homosexual advances and requests to assist with contraband, I remained clean. Some officers strongly believed that every inmate was guilty of something and deserved to be locked up. Their treatment of incarcerated women reflected their beliefs, but I tried daily to remain nonjudgmental. I needed to stay prayed up because some of the things behind those prison walls with inmates and staff alike were off the chain! In any instance when it was necessary, I didn't think twice about forming my fingers into a cross sign and pleading the blood of Jesus right in my tormentors' faces!

The inmates knew me as "Officer B" back then. I treated them as people because that was what they were regardless of the reasons for their incarceration. I always recognized that, if not for the grace of God, I could easily have been the one outfitted in green or brown instead of the respected blue. Wise treatment of God's *"least of these"* (Matthew 25: 35–40) served me well when new inmates filtered in and tested me to see how I would respond.

Thankfully, I never once had to prove anything using my hands or lethal weapons. On more than one occasion, a group of inmates, or "ladies," as I called them, seemed to appear out of nowhere when I was in a potential pinch. They blocked verbal or possible physical attacks from other inmates who ignorantly tried to test me. They would check disrespect towards me at the front door with, "Unt un, Sweetie, you got the *wronggg* one now! That's Ms. B, so you best go sit down somewhere before I have to go lay down in seg, which I don't mind doing for Ms. B because she's good people!" God had positioned unlikely allies to rise and help Jackie in the joint.

I understood how officers could become tired of hearing so many incarcerated people declare, "I'm innocent!" and "Man, I was set up!" As a Christian, however, I disagreed with the negative attitudes of many callous officers toward the inmates. Having a quart-sized Ziploc bag of cocaine placed into my pocketbook when I was unaware of it caused me to extend grace to others. I would not have believed some of the stories I heard without that firsthand experience. There is a great possibility that I would not have been as compassionate as needed for my mission at FCCW. In the volatile correctional environment, sometimes, inmates were dehumanized, and there were power struggles among staff. Sadly, I sometimes had to watch out for other officers more than I did for those with state identification numbers.

I wanted to quit every day, but God kept saying, "Not yet." One saving grace was that I had gained a notable reputation among the inmates as a good officer who was firm, fair, and consistent. Depending on the situation, I could be as kind as a kitten or as firm as a steel beam. My ability to stand toe to toe with a challenger was proven the day I walked through B dorm and heard my birth name being called loudly. I turned around and stared into the face of Lisa, a former gang member, who was incarcerated at the prison. After she jumped down from the top bunk, I thought for a moment she wanted a fight. Looking me up and down, Lisa sneered at me with scornful disdain and loudly exclaimed, "How in the HELL did you get in here with that uniform on?! You were doing the same **** things I was doing in those streets!"

Rather than looking around at those watching to see what would happen, I calmly greeted Lisa. In a respectful yet assertive voice and with a single nod, I responded,

> Hello, Lisa. I am sorry to see you here, but my name is Officer Battle, and that's how you will always address me. I know we used to run together doing the same things, but that was a *longgg* time ago. I've grown up and changed my ways. I have a criminal justice degree. Unfortunately, it seems that you haven't changed your ways yet, and that's why we're in the

same place at the same time but wearing different uniforms. Have a nice day.

I walked away without flinching and never looked back at her or the crowd.

No matter how horrific the acts they committed that landed them in prison, sometimes for life, the women inmates recognized that I didn't judge them. I always understood that their crimes were not my business. My business was custody, care, and control. Often, the women expressed gratitude and thanked me for genuinely caring for them as people versus numbers. I did so because I was a Christian although I never once promoted that. I simply lived and walked it out all over that compound every day with each person who crossed my path.

Respect-building with the inmates was undoubtedly part of God's plan to make me a fisher of men (Matthew 4:19) because my reputation drew incarcerated women to the God in me like bees to honey. *Hallelujah!* Women of all ages and ethnicities sought me out daily wherever I was on the compound. When inmates had flashbacks and meltdowns that drug-induced highs could not cover up anymore, they sent others to find me to help. Sometimes, I was delayed or could not go because of a current assignment. I would send the message, "Let them know I'm praying and will come as soon as possible!"

The Bishop of Geneva, Saint Francis de Sales, said, "To bloom where you're planted is to be content with your current circumstance and make the best of it."[2] Well, the prison was where God planted me. I learned I was created to be a light in a place of gross darkness. I realized the call to evangelism and deliverance in that space. The prison was where I learned by the spirit to transcend racial and religious prejudices. This experience taught me that the best way to dismantle bias is to deliberately unlearn previously learned behaviors.

I was a Black woman who was comfortable connecting with other Black women, and I could do that easily. However, connecting with women of different ethnicities was foreign to me beyond necessary work interactions. There were formidable walls that I simply didn't know how to scale. While in the prison system, I learned how to love women who looked nothing like me.

As the dorm officer for hundreds of women at a time, I had to respond quickly to issues and emergencies. If a Caucasian, Latina, or Asian woman under my supervision had an emotional breakdown, I had to acknowledge it without hesitation. If an atheist, Jehovah's Witness, or Rastafarian woman had a medical emergency, I had to respond without delay. No matter what, I had to respond in the right way. The correctional academy rule of thumb was "always be firm, fair, and consistent." Spending time in the prison system broadened my narrow-minded thinking regarding others. I learned how to see people with an enlightened perspective *"and leap over"* (Psalm 18:29) the walls of prejudice in my heart. That training season helped build me up to assist others without seeing any color other than red. Jesus's blood was red, and I learned that that was all that mattered. As I ministered to women in their pain and consoled them the best way that I was allowed to, I was conscious that every tear was clear, without color.

My Spirit-led humanitarian responses propelled me into another realm, and just like that, I was nervously leading women to Christ left and right almost daily! In every instance, I would pray internally: "Lord, please don't let me get caught. They will surely fire me, and I need my state job and benefits!" Nevertheless, like Queen Esther, I was determined to help those women break free from darkness however high the stakes were (Esther 4:25).

My natural job title was "correctional officer," and I was responsible for supervising the daily activities of inmates. My spiritual job title was "fisherman." My sole duty was to win lost souls at all costs. In the same manner that my shero, Harriet Tubman, stealthily escorted slaves to freedom under the cloak of darkness, I reeled in every "fish" the Holy Spirit put on the line. There were so many that I eventually lost count. Oh, I had the evangelical time of my life! To God be the glory, fishing was fast, furious, and FUN! Oh, my GOD, what joy to fill the nets for Jesus Christ!

The women received the salvation invitation so often that I could hardly keep up! They whispered, "Yes," to the invitation to accept Christ while relaxing, drinking coffee, and smoking cigarettes in the dayroom. Some said, "Yes," as they read a book or listened to music while sitting on their cots. At the back of the dorms, others uncontrollably fell to their knees. They yielded to the Holy Spirit's power in the open yards and waved white flags of surrender in the laundry rooms. A few inmates even accepted Christ during strip searches in the shower! Lord have mercy!

This witnessing activity was completely against the rules. Had someone reported it, I would have been in big trouble. I knew this very well, yet I could not stop even if I wanted to, which I didn't because I *wanted* to be used mightily by God.

Sergeants and lieutenants commended me for doing my correctional duties well, and I appreciated that. In between duties, however, I strategically navigated through that compound like an undercover FBI agent. My mission was to stop folks from going to hell in a handbasket by any means necessary. Since I had a burning desire to win souls for Christ, I seized every opportunity I could (Jeremiah 20:9). My immediate response to the sure leading was a quick, Madea-like prayer to God, asking Him to make us invisible. Occasionally, I felt I should stop taking risks; but I couldn't. Like Harriet Tubman, I worked at lightning speed, confident that I was walking with the Lord. Praise His holy name. He always came through, and we never lost a passenger. Not once was I interrupted until after the soul had accepted salvation.

What an exciting time it was! I still hated the volatile position, so I kept asking the Lord to release me from that hell hole. Understanding why I was at the prison, I promised to return to FCCW and volunteer at the earliest opportunity if I was permitted to find another job. Soon after I made that promise, God released me, and I kept my word. After attending the next volunteer orientation six months later, I volunteered with Women's Aglow for eight years. Although that was a good teaching backdrop, I was not satisfied.

Knowing there was more I needed to do, I prayed for a better way to reach souls that would allow me to release my creative juices effectively and powerfully. I received divine instructions and created a proposal to make a more significant impact at Fountain Correctional Center for Women. Favor preceded me.

The superintendent and assistant superintendent listened to what I had to say and reviewed the packages I had prayerfully and professionally prepared. They told me they loved the delicious blend of spiritual and practical training that the BuildUP! Empowerment Seminars would offer. Lord have mercy! They fired a series of questions at me when the presentation concluded: *When do you want to start? How many would you like in attendance? What schedule would you like? Where do you want to set up? What do you need from us?* It was a dream come true (Matthew 7:6–8).

Following God's pattern, creating the plan, and my former track record contributed to our benefitting from incredible favor to form the BuildUP! Empowerment training team. In the 10 years that followed, I was blessed to serve alongside many incredible women from all walks of life, *"turning the prison upside down"* (Acts 17:6). The exemplary, fearless leadership assistance of Sharon Graves and Annette Scott will remain in my memory forever. The Holy Spirit divinely connected us during different seasons to share the love of Christ throughout the facility until the doors closed.

That Ziploc bag full of cocaine and the glimpse I got of life behind prison bars were part of a much bigger purpose! I did "get life," but not in the way Satan planned. I thank God for allowing me to see His hand move mightily for 18 years in open salvations, deliverances, miracles, signs, and wonders that remain testimonies today.

*Unlikely allies
are positioned
to rise &
help.*

denied
transitive verb
di·naid

1: to declare (something) to be untrue, 2: to refuse to admit or acknowledge (something), 4: to refuse to accept the existence, truth, or validity of[1]

CHAPTER 8

DENIED: THE CLOCK HAD STOPPED

I hate cancer. I hate cancer. I. HATE. CANCER. Mama had been battling cancer for five years. She epitomized the notion of being long-suffering and *"endured hardness as a good soldier"* (2 Timothy 2:3–4) in a way that I would never have thought possible for a human being. I never accepted it when she gathered my siblings and me to tell us about the diagnosis. My faith meter shot up to the top of the charts and stayed there. I prayed, fasted, and confessed; I warred in the spirit. I refused to speak anything other than life about her outcome. I restricted access to her by anyone who spoke or even exuded anything else. I consistently prayed and quoted healing scriptures (Isaiah 38:16, Isaiah 53:5, Psalm 30:2) for her healing every day from the beginning.

Fueling those decrees was gratefulness that even though Mama and I had started with a pain-heavy relationship, it had not remained that way. Hallelujah! When I was 21, God began turning the Titanic around as a result of prayer and genuine efforts to salvage the relationship. When I heard my Mama say she loved me for the first time, I was 27, but it didn't matter. Mama had said it! God helped me understand that she was an amazing woman who had raised me the best she could, the best she knew. Since she was a victim of adverse childhood experiences, drama, and trauma herself—as corroborated by multiple siblings in numerous ways—this reframing was impressive. The Holy Spirit and combined human service and mental health employment backgrounds taught me that environmental shaping and learned behaviors tended to be transmitted through the womb, ultimately influencing everyday experiences. Therefore, Mama simply replicated what had been shown to her.

Nevertheless, God moved mightily in our relationship. It didn't happen overnight, but God and all of the heavens fought for us. He pushed back the darkness in a more extraordinary way than I ever could have imagined. Our broken relationship became incredibly BEAUTIFUL! When God stopped working on us, we had forgiven each other for all real and perceived wrongs. We were a redemptive testimony of the manifested promise of restoration for what the locusts had eaten up (Joel 2:25–26). Mama still was not the huggy type with her children, but it was okay because we knew she deeply loved us in many ways. One day I got the courage to ask her why she would let my siblings and I hug and kiss her but not return the same physical affection to us. She dropped her head, shrugged her shoulders, and replied with hands lifted in internal bewilderment, "I honestly don't know, but I'm so glad to see that you are different from me in that way with Jawaan and Marquaysa." I accepted her response and her love languages without further questions.

By His grace, Mama and I became the absolute best of friends who updated each other on the phone several times a week, just talking and laughing about whatever. We had keys to each other's homes. It was nothing for me to arrive home and find her curled up on my couch asleep like Goldilocks, and I would cover her with a blanket and let her get her rest. Oh, my goodness! We regularly enjoyed all kinds of local mother-daughter outings. At 50, she took her first and only plane trip with me to Florida to board the Carnival cruise ship. We were so excited about the opportunity to explore the beautiful Bahama islands together and enjoyed ourselves tremendously.

While we were growing up, Mama did not give us the option of *not* attending church and Bible study if we lived in her home. She regularly gave us no choice but to go to church, participate every time she said so, and do it with smiles on our faces. We sometimes didn't like it, but that consistent exposure planted Christian seeds inside us. Mama made me—yes, *made me*—serve with the youth, sing in the choir, and make a speech every time the church announced an upcoming program. I became an avid reader and wordsmith due to my mama's insatiable love for reading magazines and books by the stacks. Much later, I realized that my teaching ability stemmed from her too. She modeled incredible housecleaning, work, bill-paying, and green thumb ethics that set a high standard I have followed most of my life. She is why I learned to love serving in outreach ministry, feeding the homeless, and visiting people in prison to share the love of Christ.

Life went on, and cancer was something we lived above and despite for the most part. The years rolled by with a lot of intentional good times. However, in the fifth year, the pressure mounted, and her cancer suddenly became more real and immediate. It was in our faces like a nasty black fly that wouldn't go away. We swatted at the cancer with Scripture instead of a typical plastic fly swatter. I knew Mama had good and bad days, but I saw the cancer's true magnitude after I moved into her home to assist with caretaking. Although we had very regular contact, she had masked her pain well during waking hours. The night pain was a different animal that insisted on being heard and seen.

I can't tell you how many nights I knelt by her bedside all night long, pleading for the blood of Jesus to help her. I quoted healing Scriptures and played soft music. I laid my hands on her body as she writhed uncontrollably, moaning and groaning. There are no words to describe the ceaseless ordeal of warring and interceding for her to find relief from intense physical pain and suffering. Hurt burned in my heart for her. To this day, 16 years later, I have never seen anything like the suffering I saw Mama endure once I moved in as a caregiver. She lived life out loud, taking each moment as it came, and I never heard a complaint from her.

I will never forget the day we had a candid conversation in the living room while she sat in her favorite blue recliner with the padded armrests and brown pull handle on the left side. With shoulders shrugged and hands raised, she quietly yet tearfully shared that she did not want to die but it was not up to her to decide. I passionately encouraged her to have faith and speak life. Mama remained a trooper. However, the inhumane suffering increased rapidly to the point that I knew something had to change, especially when she told me on a different day in a shaky but resigned voice, "I want to die." Not wanting to upset her, I said nothing out loud, but I simply could not accept it. I became even angrier with the forces of hell and waged war in the spirit realm. I could not, would NOT lose her now when we were just getting started!

Later that evening, I knelt beside that same blue chair she had sat in when making that confession, and I cried out to God that she was just understandably worn out. I interceded for a genuine miracle as only He could grant. As I bombarded heaven with prayers and petitions, I was shocked to see an evil spirit the size of a smurf enter the room. It came up behind me and lifted a brick to strike me in the back of my head.

As I write, I am reminded that I used to rap under the name Smurfette. Wow! The enemy tried to demonize me to make me stop praying for my mama, but it didn't work. All I could say at that moment was, "Jesus!" That one-word arrow prayer hit the bullseye. The evil spirit evaporated into thin air as I gave God praise instead of shrinking back in fear.

Despite the attempt to silence me, my faith that I would receive a miracle for Mama never wavered. Instead, my confidence grew, and during the growth process, I became wiser. My selfish prayers changed into prayers of surrender. I loved MAMA enough to want her to be free one way or the other. I understood that if God did not choose to heal her on this side of heaven, He would indeed heal her on the other side. That strengthened me to pray the way Jesus did when He knew what needed to be done but wished for another answer (Luke 22:42).

As a nurse in the oncology ward, Mama had been familiar with chronic critical illness and had known the ebb and flow. Mama used to say, "There is no need for anybody to walk around in pain with all this God-given medicine out here!" Consequently, she took her daily meds. Chapel Hill and Rocky Mount doctor visits were regular occurrences in her life. Hospital visits had become an occasional necessity so that Mama could receive and regroup from a blood transfusion. Sometimes, she bounced back faster than she did other times. One particular time, Mama gave me quite a scare with the length of her stay. Just when it seemed she was coming home, there was an exhausting setback. Among the most unforgettable nights of my life was the night when I sat alone in my car in the hospital parking lot after finishing a visit and came completely unglued as I fought for her life in the spirit realm.

With an anguished soul and fearful heart, I sat there blubbering, raging, and shaking my fist at God because it looked like I was losing my mama. Though I kept praying, fasting, and confessing my faith, I could feel I was losing her, and we needed more time! Through tears, I begged God to please just heal her. While wiping snot away with my sweater sleeve, I bargained with some of everything if He would prevent the death angels from taking her and let her stay with us. Mercifully, I wasn't struck down right there in the car. Heaven heard me, and Mama rallied yet again. She held on for a while but returned to the fifth floor again a few months later.

Jawaan graduated from high school on a Friday night with his regular, fully earned diploma. Afterward, we went by the hospital so Mama could see his graduation attire and the full-scale diploma he had earned despite his learning disability. She was so happy and proud of her first grandchild! Before Mama had gone to the hospital, I had decided to take the kids on an overnight trip to Emerald Pointe Waterpark in Greensboro, North Carolina, for Jawaan's graduation gift on Saturday. After gassing up the car with the kids and my godsister, Tammie, we stopped by to check on Mama and let her know the plan. The previous week, she had improved, and the doctor had said he'd probably release her by Tuesday. Lord have mercy. As soon as I walked into the hospital room, I saw that the clock on the wall had stopped. I quickly closed my eyes and told myself it was nothing. Deep inside, my spirit knew what it meant, but my soul said, "No, no, no, not so!" She appeared to be struggling, and I couldn't understand how things had changed so much overnight.

Although I was worried about leaving town, Jawaan's accomplishments needed to be celebrated. Mama would want that for him, and since it was just one night, I decided that we should go and come straight back. The nurses promised to call me immediately if necessary after I told them where I was going.

We reached our DoubleTree hotel room but never set foot inside the Waterpark. The park trip didn't materialize because, as fate would have it, the hospital called later that night. The sweet head nurse softly and slowly said, "Jackie, I'm sorry, but I think you need to get here as soon as possible. Please know that Nan will not be alone if you don't make it in time." The nurses caring for my mom in the Oncology Ward were not only her respected colleagues but also dear friends who deeply loved her. I knew they would be there holding her hand, but I needed to be the one there holding her hand.

Immediately, we packed up our things, put on the hazard lights, and drove Lexy-Gurl up I-40 E at a record-breaking speed. Upon arriving at Nash General Hospital, I flew inside and—except while we were in the elevator—didn't stop running until I reached my mama's room. As I approached her bedside, I picked up her right hand, which was cool to the touch, squeezed it tightly, and began doing what I knew to do. I fervently prayed, asking God to turn her bleak status around again as He had done so many times before. It was not to be this time. While I was holding her hand, tears began to fall from my eyes differently because suddenly, I realized that I was selfishly holding her spirit hostage. I could no longer do it, so I told her how much I loved her and hated seeing her in such pain. The next words out of my mouth were "Mama, it's okay. If you are ready to go now, then you go. We'll be alright."

My precious mama departed this world the next day around noon. I saw and heard her take her last breath, which shattered my heart into shards like broken glass. Standing there by that bed, I sobbed until I was breathless. I had been sure this would simply be another hospital stay. I would have done anything, given my all, for that to have been the case, but it hadn't been. Without warning, the clock stopped, and my mama was gone. Unbelievably, at 38 years of age, I lost her. That was heartbreakingly tough, yet the day of the homegoing was infinitely worse. Pain washed over me like waves in the ocean as I dressed and readied myself to attend Mama's homegoing service. Unable to accept that this was happening, I slowly dressed in the tan Kasper skirt suit she had gifted me with for Christmas just six months before.

As soon as I looked at my Sunday best ready-to-go self in the mirror, I began to feel dreadfully sick to the pit of my stomach. It flipped, causing me to wretch uncontrollably. I tried not to cry and mess up my makeup as I ran for the trash can to catch the vomit that was seconds away from flying out of my mouth. Tammie was in the bedroom with me for support. She laid her hands on my stomach and prayed for the Holy Spirit to help me make it through the homegoing service. Tammie patted my face with tissues and brought me water. I will always thank God for that kindness.

Music has permanently moved me. Somehow a specific tune always assigns itself to my situations, whether I am experiencing victory or pain. As we were en route to church in the family car, a tune rose to meet me. In 1971, Bill Withers released a song entitled "Ain't No Sunshine."[2] That song infiltrated my spirit. A portion of the timeless lyrics follow:

> Ain't no sunshine when she's gone
> It's not warm when she's away
> Ain't no sunshine when she's gone
> And she's always gone too long
> Anytime she goes away
> Wonder this time where she's gone

Wonder if she's gone to stay
Ain't no sunshine when she's gone
And this house just ain't no home
Anytime she goes away

The lyrics continue with the heartfelt repetition of "I know" a total of 26 times.

Now that Mama had gone away, no sliver of sunshine was present. As I sat through the homegoing service, a verse was on loop in my ear. It droned on when I had to walk out of the church and leave her there. I remember tearfully thinking, "See you later, Best Friend." Pain sliced through my circulation as the hearse drove me away to the committal service in the rain. I could not believe we were about to put Mama into that nasty, wet ground. What would I do without the sunshine now? I had no idea. Denial lay heavy on my heart and trying to figure it out assaulted my brain.

*Our broken
relationship
became so
incredibly beautiful!*

derailed
transitive verb
de·railed

1: to cause to run off the rails 2a: to obstruct
the progress of: FRUSTRATE,
2b: to upset the stability or composure of[1]

CHAPTER 9

DERAILED: DEVIL IN NAVY BLUE PINSTRIPE

By God's grace, we got through the searing loss of our Mama one day at a time, but everything was so different. The devil knew I still had a massive hole in my heart and did not mind filling it. The new year came in. Life was better than ever, but we were minus Mama, which was such an oxymoron. One day, as I was headed home from work, I began to feel overwhelming loneliness that increased with every mile I drove. I remember thanking God for all my blessings and still feeling derailed by sorrow.

I recall saying aloud,

> Lord seems like I've finally got the cake, but where's the icing for the cake? I have not been in a relationship in seven years! I've barely dated, and that isn't right. Lord Jesus, where is my husband? I have no one to

share life with, and I don't want to be alone anymore. Please hear my prayers, Lord, and bless me as I do the best I can to *"delight myself in you"* (Psalm 37:4). In Jesus name. Amen.

While I remembered the Word, I forgot that the devil was also an imitator who could hear and appear to answer prayers as well.

Not many days later, I had an experience like never before. Great day in the morning; it began raining men! Hallelujah! Men began approaching me every single day everywhere I went! Whoo, Wee! I couldn't believe what was happening. I was 100% sure the heavens had heard me and opened up just because I had asked. I was especially tickled because I was wearing an orthopedic boot on my right foot to heal an ankle broken in two places, but apparently, that didn't detract from my beauty.

One of the men approached me in the grocery store on a Friday afternoon and asked if I knew what aisle the apple juice was in. I told him, and a 45-minute conversation followed while we were standing in the canned goods aisle. Mason told me he was shopping for snack items for his sister's daycare. His arms were full of individually wrapped snack items, and while we spoke, he kept dropping boxes he had gathered before crossing paths with me. I eventually encouraged him to place the items in my basket while we talked.

At the end of the conversation, he pushed the basket to the counter and paid for everything in it. From the get-go, he was really good at his strategies. Unfortunately, I was unaware that my handicap was still an outward vulnerability though it didn't make me less attractive. It was a gateway to my inner vulnerability due to losing my mama. Why didn't that occur to me at the time?

Mason took my things to the car. He asked if I was in a hurry, and I replied I wasn't, so he invited me to get a quick bite to eat. We dined and talked. Over dinner, he told me positive things about himself. To my surprise, I learned he was a pastor. I did something I'd never done with other men at our first meetings: I shared that I was an elder in the church. We laughed at the unexpected commonality. Laughing about it was much better than convincing someone that serving in ministry would not be a relationship issue. He also told me about his checkered past, a straight-up mess. In retrospect, he pulled an Eminem *8 Mile* playbook move by putting his ish on blast before someone else could.

He confessed his wrongs and the painful lessons he had learned. I remained nonjudgmental due to my background as a deliverance minister. I should have saved myself from a trip to hell by running right then. My fallacy was that I listened to foolery and gave the benefit of the doubt when I should not have. The deep sense of loss and sorrow I still carried on the inside made me susceptible to what was nothing more than a wolf in sheep's clothing.

The enemy used my total belief in deliverance and second chances against me by convoluting my common sense with the idea that my prayers were about to be answered. When we pray, the devil also hears and knows how to respond if we're willing to hear him out. I foolishly allowed Satan to sneak—no, slither—into my life when I should have appropriately distinguished the light from the darkness. Satan intended *"to steal, kill, and destroy"* (John 10:10) everything good about me. Since he had no authority to do that, he schemed to derail my destiny through this seemingly godly encounter.

The pastor and I began getting to get to know each other regularly. We discovered a mutual Christian acquaintance who said nothing but positive things about him. Soon after, I met some highly respected ministry leaders who supported him. Seeing their involvement with him further led me to accept his tale of ruin and redemption. The crazy thing is that my relationship with this man helped build up my ministry. He believed in and promoted my gifts more than I did. He constantly pushed me to soar and be great. He secured fruitful ministry engagements for me in surrounding cities. He convinced me to engage in a weekly radio broadcast. He provided resources for anything I could imagine as I executed ministry assignments. Before I could finish extracting thoughts from my preacher's imagination, he was already in motion, helping to bring them to life. I thought it was *just incredible* how he helped me in ministry. Gracious! That support was what I had hoped to experience one day. Moreover, it was what I thought I needed, making me believe God had supplied it.

I must admit that sometimes things sprang up during the courtship that disturbed my peace. In retrospect, they were rapidly blinking caution lights designed to make me pause. Although I struggled with internal doubts, I glossed over the truth and kept riding the train. More than once, I ministered to the necessity to *"Get wisdom though it cost all you have"* (Proverbs 4:7, NIV). It taught that each of us was responsible for staying in the realm of wisdom. If only I had stood on that instead of falling for his bull jive. Sadly, the silly girl in me was anything but wise. She knew but didn't *"seek peace and pursue it"* (Psalm 34:14).

I was not as sharp as I needed to be in matters of the heart. Love was something that I had always searched for but seemed unable to find. Unfortunately, I had not grown up with any godly examples of positive relationships. Deep inside, I could periodically hear Mama's words echoing in my soul: "You see, that's your problem. You always love all the wrong people!" Those scalding hot words were indelibly etched into my heart, mind, and spirit. Perhaps she was right after all because it seemed I was reliving that declaration again. Sigh!

Common sense would have been my saving grace had I let it. I had spiritually learned scripture on what God said about godly relationships, yet I fluctuated in and out of peace with this man. I would have it then lose it, have it then lose it. Once I obtained it, I didn't ensure it remained consistent. That was the key! I ignorantly settled for flighty peace instead of constant peace. Despite my disappointment, I should not have walked away but run away faster than Forrest Gump did the day he ran from his bullies!

One way or another, God will make sure necessary information is conveyed. My daughter introduced me to a very influential online relationship expert years ago. Her unshakable belief was that a man should be measured, not by what he said, but by what he did. And it had to be consistent, or it was a wrap. I missed the power of that belief. My longing for what I thought would fulfill me resulted in total derailment. He was not eloquent at all; however, he was incredibly persuasive. He lived a double life and was the kind of person committed to holding on to a lie until Jesus's return. The man was a narcissistic master manipulator.

The devil knew exactly how to spin it to get my attention. He made sure the pastor wore navy blue pinstripe suits and could recite the entire Bible. His strength—"the ability to recite the Bible flawlessly"—was what I perceived as one of my areas of weakness and impressed me more than anything else. Nevertheless, my ignorance was anything but bliss. What I thought was a dream come true turned out to be a "nightmare on Elm Street" that I couldn't seem to escape. I had allowed myself to love him despite his past. That foolish decision to entertain *"bad fruit"* (Matthew 12:33) derailed every aspect of my life.

Mason leased a church three months before our wedding, and I was ordained as a pastor. Shortly after, his true colors began to emerge. In a fit of frustration, this man alongside whom I willingly co-pastored openly revealed that he was jealous of my anointing and ministry ability. Angry, he audaciously said, "I wish God would just TAKE your anointing and give it to me!"

I was stunned to see how serious he was. For about a minute and a half, I looked him right in the eyes, brows furrowed. Finally, I assured him with assertiveness and certainty, "You know what? Wishing is good, but wishing will never, ever make that happen. You must work with what you have been given just like I do, so get over it!" I reminded him that he wasn't graced for the same assignments as I was and vice versa. It didn't help one bit. When the covering apostle carefully and prayerfully suggested I become the church's lead pastor instead of co-pastor, he grew more bitter and jealous. Mason's bitterness skyrocketed when he heard the belief that the ministry would grow more with me as the leader and him as the overseer. It resulted in him experiencing physical sickness; he was bedridden for days.

The marriage continued on its questionable course: When an Amtrak train running at 100 mph derails, the only possible result is a massive train wreck. After the explosive crash, I thought I'd never rise from beneath the mess. Here, I am suddenly reminded that not long after he asked me to marry him, I had a dream in which I was at a giant garage sale. I was about to purchase an item of interest when something in the rear corner suddenly caught my attention. I went closer to see what it was. It was a giant white Christmas tree with endless sparkling lights, which I had always dreamed of having! Despite its beauty, I resisted buying it at the last minute because the cost of the artificial tree was too high.

Lordy! It was a prophetic warning about marrying him, but I misunderstood the red flags. One contribution to my misunderstanding was that Jawaan shared a dream with me before the wedding. He said he dreamed that "Grandma was standing at the altar behind the other ladies, holding a big bunch of colorful flowers, and she was smiling." Encouragement blossomed in my heart like that bouquet, but it was a pseudo-justification for what my heart wanted to be true. I continued riding the train to a beautiful marriage altar with no idea how drastically it would *alter* my whole world in a negative sense.

On the other hand, my prophetic dream was an accurate arrow that hit the bullseye. Being in a relationship with this pastor almost cost me everything. Before I connected with him, my career was on track, money was a non-issue, and the ministry was already flowing well. Two weeks earlier, I had successfully spearheaded my first women's conference, "Designed With Destiny In Mind," totally by faith; over 300 women had attended it by the end of the second day.

The pastor was by my side every step of the way, helping make it happen. What a contradiction it was for him to help build a victory and then help the enemy tear it down. I didn't recall that if someone enabled you to do a good thing, it didn't necessarily mean they were godsent. I missed the "best through" part of the expiration date because the more delicate print underneath the fine print was too small for my eyes. I missed the "no return, no refund" policy notice before buying that truckload of horse manure!

Things finally hit the fan via the arrival of a letter in my mailbox. I now recall that God sent me a sign of what I was about to get myself into about a month before that letter arrived. Another church was courting us to become its lead pastors. On a Sunday, we were asked to administer the Holy Communion, which I was very honored to do. Per custom, the taking of the Lord's Supper was introduced with the contextual reading (I Corinthians 11:23–25). I had served the Holy Communion countless times; however, that day was different. When I heard, "This is My body, which is broken for you," I felt like something had gut-punched me, and I doubled over. Suddenly, I was knocked into spiritual turmoil and knew something was breaking. I was preparing for another level of warfare rather than overseeing another church.

Warfare in the form of an anonymous letter arrived in my home mailbox the following month. The opening line read: "Please know that I am very sorry that this is happening to you." Someone insisted they were writing to me because they believed me to be a good, godly woman who had a right to know that the man I was married to was not who he appeared to be. According to the person, my husband, Pastor Mason, was plotting to kill me. The letter said he had been setting it up for months by telling people that I was slowly dying from an illness we were keeping under wraps. He said it might not look like it, but I did not have a very long time left to live. My eyes widened as I read the letter. I felt the train vibrations run through me; however, allowing no tears to fall, I plowed on to the next page.

The letter went on to say that he was sleeping with two of our female church members, one of whom I had believed to be my dear friend for over a decade. It stated that multiple women had been told they would soon be his next wife. As if that were not enough, the letter said that he was also financially ripping off our church members and others in the community with fake real estate deals. People were distraught at realizing they had wholeheartedly placed trust in their pastor and in return, he had grievously mangled that trust with manipulation and theft.

Before saying a word to him about receiving the letter, I prayed for days. Then I took the letter to the Sheriff's Department to see if I could press premeditation charges against him. I was advised that the anonymous letter was insufficient proof to process anything. Next, I quietly began a strategic investigation. Surprisingly because it was so long ago, I recalled how I had devoured the Nancy Drew mystery book series as a kid and how her sleuthing abilities had fascinated me. Taking courage from that memory, I drove my little red Kia Rio to the first stop on my route. I made sure to arrive unannounced to catch everyone off guard. I walked up to individuals as the Holy Spirit led me to, looked them in the eyes with a smile, and softly said, "The Lord says you have something to tell me. What is it?"

Everyone, male and female alike, immediately opened up and revealed what I knew to be the truth, the whole truth, and nothing but the truth. Relieved to unload heavy burdens, some couldn't stop talking. They were glad to tell me and hoped I could help them if they were victims of financial fraud. Some asked for forgiveness for not expressing concern earlier as they pulled out phones to show me extensive text messages. Others cried as they confessed that they were aware of his schemes and that they were being pressured to conceal them.

As I made my rounds, I listened and prayed for people as necessary. I erased their fears that spiritual involvements with their pastor were unacceptable to God. I explained that the gifts of God were without repentance. I assured several that their salvation was genuine. A couple of parents were assured that baby dedications were pure. I came within moments of beating my former friend down to the ground when she challenged me about her mess during the ordeal. Fifteen years of friendship were poured down the drain like a can of Drano. By the grace of God through Jesus Christ, I kept my hands to myself the day we had the confrontation in a parking lot. Even though my head and heart were screaming compound cuss words, I did not let them come out of my mouth.

I continued the investigation. After gathering my facts, I did not confront this man I had married alone. As a precaution, I requested we visit a close godly couple to avoid the chaos after Pandora's box opened wide. For my safety, I revealed the letter and my findings there, which I knew to be factual, and my prediction of his response was spot on. Once I confronted him and our fellow pastors objectively assessed the situation, this self-professed "Man of God" that I was married to unraveled right before me.

Interestingly, he was more upset that I appeared calm than anything else. Sitting there, I watched multiple personality disorder (MPD) emerge from hibernation. It was hideous. The narcissistic liar in him denied every bit of it. He declared he was being set up and couldn't believe that I thought that letter full of lies was true. Like a madman, he stormed out of the home after refusing objective spiritual counsel.

On our way back home, those demons awoke from a state of dormancy and went entirely OFF! As I drove, he hollered, screamed, and beat the air like a crazed lunatic. Recalling the scriptures, I thought about the behavior of the man who called himself *"Legions, for we are many"* (Mark 5:6–10). Jesus! I feared for my safety yet refused to allow those spirits of rage to see me sweat. Inwardly, the locomotive was grinding to a screeching halt. Externally, I did not shed a single teardrop. I prayed in tongues silently the whole way home and audibly throughout the night.

Every day revealed more mayhem that this master demonic spirit had caused. Various stories of pastoral abuse and manipulation emerged from the woodwork. Law enforcement got involved once his criminal acts hit the news and he fled the city to elude arrest. Bail bondsmen harassed me incessantly, refusing to believe I was not hiding Pastor Mason inside. One Sunday afternoon, I suddenly heard a loud banging on my front door. A man's deep voice yelled at me to open the door immediately.

I ran to the door, and our pit bull, Tyson, followed me to see who it was. I told the bail bondsman to give me a minute to put the dog away. As he banged on my door, he yelled and cursed. He warned me that he was "about to kick the door in if I didn't open it RIGHT NOW!" Instead of trying to put the dog away, I snatched the door open and saw a madman pointing a gun at me. He kept cursing at me and refused to identify himself by name. Seeing no badge, I refused him entry because I did not trust him.

Instead, I picked up the phone and dialed the Sheriff's office on speakerphone. I explained who I was and what was presently happening. They already knew the backdrop because I had communicated and cooperated with them from day one. They advised me they were sending me assistance and staying with me on speakerphone, which infuriated the bail bondsman. With his gun still pointed at me, he called me a *****. Suddenly, I had had ENOUGH! Righteous indignation rose in me, and simultaneously, I felt angelic hosts all around me. It was softly impressed on my spirit, "If he takes one step over this threshold, he will immediately drop dead." I fully believed God would do what He said. By then, I was so frustrated and angry with the bail bondsman that I wanted to see that happen.

I threw the door open as wide as possible and said, "You keep disrespecting me to my face here at my own home. You dare to call me out of my name when I have done nothing wrong. You know what?! Come in! I have decided that I WANT you to come in." I stepped aside and held Tyson back with my left hand. With my right hand, I motioned to him to come on inside several times with a smile on my face. He stiffened and just looked at me. He did not, however, take a single step over my threshold. I couldn't help but laugh out loud.

After all that disrespectful drama, the big bad wolf didn't even make an "about to move" gesture. Still holding Tyson and keeping the door open, I gestured with my head for him to come on in. Without another mumbling word, he put away the gun, walked off the front porch of my home, and left before the Sheriff's Department arrived. God had truly "given His angels charge over me" (Psalm 91:11–12). I was glad a dead body didn't have to be pulled out of my home because Tyson and I still had to live there.

During one of the midweek bounty hunter pop-up visits, I was shocked and frightened to walk past the window and see that while two men were searching inside my home, another man was posted in my backyard. He had been underneath my home, checking the crawl space, and was also there in case the fugitive tried to make a run for it. These men were not rude or disrespectful, and I saw their observance of the genuine fear I exhibited when I saw that man in the yard. My once peaceful home remained under surveillance for a long time. No matter what I said, the bail bondsman remained convinced that he was hiding inside. So it went until suddenly, it all just stopped. Why? I didn't know and was so glad to have my peace restored that I didn't care or question it.

Admittedly, I had made a terrible mistake. I had ignorantly aligned myself with evil by marrying a pathological liar and whole live sociopath. I didn't know it then, but that gave the enemy legal authority to derail my train! I had loved him on purpose with eyes that I had thought were wide open but were blinded. God mercifully lifted the thick scales off my eyes to help me see correctly. As I see it, God made my blindness work for my good (Romans 8:28). I say this because the blindness—which was actually ignorance—allowed me to be hedged in and kept me from being an accessory to his plethora of criminal acts. Letting that marriage fall to the ground and die was very disappointing, but once I saw what I saw and knew what I knew, it was easy to shut it down.

I filed for divorce as soon as possible, but because of his flight status, it cost more money and took longer to finalize the divorce and remove his name from the property. Oh my God, that was the most terrible season! I don't know what happened to that sociopath and I never once tried to find out. As far as I was concerned, he was dead. Although he was physically gone, he had caused so much mental and emotional trauma that I was left with psychological damage.

Spiritual warfare had been unleashed upon my life by the enemy, and it was such a complex season of overwhelming loss. The marriage had been busted wide open with a professed "compassionate" letter. As a result of that broken rail, several more popped loose. I lost what I considered to be one of my two best friends. I lost a church congregation that meant so much to me. I lost my identity as a ministry leader. I lost ministry opportunities that had been on the calendar for ages because people didn't want to be associated with a mess. I lost confidence in friends when I saw one turn around and walk away rather than face me when they didn't know I had seen them. Walls made of glass are excellent reflectors—gifts from God.

Within weeks, I was further devastated when the job that had recently promoted me to supervisor terminated me without warning. They gave me a list of fabricated reasons that attacked my character and work performance, which I refuted. About six months later, I received confirmation from a reliable source that I was only an innocent scapegoat.

My seemingly smooth-running train derailed within four short months. The result was a mangled mess, and every compartment toppled over. It felt like I had been in a terrible accident and had simultaneously broken my back, neck, right arm, and right leg. I know that's a bit dramatic; however, the train wreck was more than a metaphor to me. It was my reality, and multiple rails were fractured, some irreparably. Here I am reminded of a nursery rhyme:

> Humpty Dumpty sat on a wall,
> Humpty Dumpty had a great fall.
> All the king's horses and all the king's men
> Couldn't put Humpty together again.[2]

It was too much; I had fallen and couldn't get up. Or so I thought. Like Humpty, I was still obviously cracked and fractured. There didn't seem to be any Band-Aids big enough this time around. I will never forget the day the dam finally broke in the therapist's office. For what seemed like hours, I cried uncontrollably. It felt like I was losing my last tiny piece of mind this time. I didn't want to continue trying anymore. As soon as I arrived home, my compassionate daughter inquired about the visit. Unable to say a single word, I merely shook my head from side to side. The tears threatened to return as I closed the door to my bedroom. The grueling session had taken the wind out of my sails. I couldn't catch my breath at that moment.

Before I could put a butt print on the bed, the door opened, and my then 19-year-old daughter, Marquaysa, who stood almost a foot taller than me, entered the room. Without a word, she swooped me up from the bed where I sat in utter despair, again just moments away from the edge of the ledge. She wrapped me in her arms and began rubbing my hair and back. Then she began to pray over me. Marquaysa did not pray some cute little "Lord, please help my mama" prayer. Talk about a return on investment for the fruits of my parental laboring. The roles had been divinely switched!

My only beloved daughter reversed the chase on the enemy (2 Samuel 23:20), warred in the spirit, and commanded dark despair to break off me immediately! She demanded my release from dark torment and restitution for every tear I shed. She took authority over the tormenting spirits of brokenness, shame, pain, and self-condemnation. With no fear, in a battle cry voice I had never heard before, she told them all to "Go BACK to the pits of hell in Jesus' mighty name." She meant every word she said and loosed healing, peace, and strength *for* me. I've never forgotten that day she went to the gates of hell on my behalf. She's not my mini-me; she's one of the best parts of me, for which I'm beyond blessed.

From the moment Marquaysa Lacell Battle was placed in my arms at birth, I began interceding for her. I declared that she would never wonder if I truly loved her. I broke and renounced the generational curse of teen pregnancy because that counterfeit buck stopped with me. I decreed that she would never allow herself to be inhumanely treated by anyone. As I held her in my arms, I prayed that she would forever receive all of God's blessings so she could stand and have an overall better life. I decreed that she would be all she was predestined to be to the glory of God *without* unnecessary trauma. She helped me heal through that season and never once judged me.

Guess who also helped me recover from that traumatic fiasco. Mama! Extremely late one night, after I had cried myself to sleep, I sensed a presence in the room and sat straight up in the bed. Mama's spirit was sitting on the side of the bed. As soon as I realized it was her, I began to cry. My mama immediately moved closer, wrapped me in her arms, and held me tight. Just as Marquaysa had done, she rubbed my hair and compassionately patted my back. While I cried, her arms tightly encircled me, as one would do with a helpless child. Without saying a word,

Mama *physically and emotionally* mothered me after death as she never had in life. That visitation was a gift from God, and it gave me the one thing I had always wanted more than anything: to feel my mama's love physically and tangibly.

That dream helped me heal. I learned firsthand that healing right was an inside-out job, not an outside-in job. It also had to run its entire course. Similar to the world's ongoing efforts to overcome the COVID-19 pandemic, healing and recovery after a train wreck is never a quick, bounce-right-back situation. In my case, it was a detailed process that had a set time. I couldn't do it alone, so God mercifully sent me help. The precious godsister who helped me bear my mama's homegoing was there. My beautiful butterfly of a daughter was there. An excellent Christian therapist was there. Each of them played a pivotal role in helping me rise from beneath the mangled multiple-train wreck.

*It can look like
what you prayed
for, but is it really
GOD?!*

defeated
noun
de·feat·ed

1: the state of being beaten or having lost
2: To prevent the success of; thwart[1]

CHAPTER 10

DEFEATED: SELF-IMPOSED BLINDNESS

Try as I might, I simply could not remain in the light to the degree that I should have been able to. Wasn't I an ordained evangelist, teacher, and pastor? For decades I had been teaching and preaching deliverance to others. However now it was me who needed them. Who can the encourager turn to when in need of encouragement? Where does the wounded warrior go when she needs chronic wound care? Where does the one called and chosen to deliver others by the power of God go when she needs to be delivered?!

Who can truly understand what a severely wounded warrior experiences when she cannot articulate it herself? When can she dare to take the bandages off and look at the scars in the mirror for the first time? How can she finally do that and not pass right out at the revolting image reflected in it? God gave me a Jack-In-The-Box-like spirit, built to keep popping back up no matter what, but it wasn't working! Instead, it seemed like the crank had given out, and the manufacturer's warranty had expired. Sigh... The proverb quoted in Luke 4:23, *"Physician, heal yourself!"* wasn't working either. I have been blessed to see miracles, signs, and wonders performed through God in me for others. Unfortunately, this warrior was out of steam, too wounded to help herself.

Hypocritical feelings compounded the feelings of defeat that encroached upon my life. I felt unable to succeed at or achieve anything to the level I had envisioned. I still looked good with makeup always laid and hair always slayed. I effortlessly dressed and drove well, switching between luxury and economy vehicles based on my daily schedule. My white teeth and bright smile drew regular compliments, but my mind was a constant battlefield. My joy was gone again because I felt incredibly defeated. I tried to hold on to hope, but my hope rope had dwindled to a thread.

All I heard were tormented taunts that I was the world's biggest fool who had miserably failed at love. Again. The voices in my head led me to focus more on the problems than the solutions. Helen Keller is known for saying, "The only thing worse than being blind is having sight but no vision."[2] As a result of my blurry vision, I became spiritually blind regarding my private world (Proverbs 29:18).

My defeated state of mind was an assault weapon against me, and I forgot that the scripture *"My grace is sufficient for you"* (2 Corinthians 12:9) was my lifeline. I'd publicly referenced it to pull, pray, preach, and prophesy broken women through train wrecks 1,000 times! So why did I struggle to get myself out of tricky situations? I am reminded of the scene in the movie, *Ray*, where the title character was in rehab and his mother's spirit visited him. She spoke powerful words that gave him the strength to face his heroin addiction demons head-on. Her stern yet loving words reminded him that "she had told him not to become a cripple, but he had become one anyway." His eyes filled with tears of shame after the soul-stirring sting helped him realize what he had allowed himself to become.

Ray's addiction was a result of his actions. My self-imposed spiritual blindness was similar. I allowed it to make me more of a disabled person than I had been in the wheelchair at 16 years. Much later in life, there were many times when I couldn't get up all the way emotionally or psychologically. It seemed as though leaping over or around three landmines landed me into five more. I would never have made it if I had not periodically heard a voice calling my name, reminding me of my purpose and destiny. Without it, I would be sitting in a corner in a white room, wearing a white straitjacket while rocking back and forth, incoherent, and unreachable.

During those days, I felt like I couldn't help myself, couldn't reclaim myself. Dramatic and traumatic events seemed to be attracted to me like iron to a magnet. This resulted in my feeling that I was damaged goods and irreparably broken on the inside. I was sad about my life's direction, and my head hurt from trying to figure out how to redirect it. Yep, I was mighty confused, and you know what else? I was also furious that this happened when I thought I was finally winning. Outwardly, I continued to appear to be holding my head above water. Internally, I was constantly gulping for the next breath of fresh air.

The shocking thing was that the ministry kept calling my broken vessel at an increased rate. My primary concern was that I wanted to hear God's voice telling me what to say and needed to minister without contaminating people with my pain. As soon as I received an invitation, I began fasting and praying.

Regardless of the facts, the fiery embers of ministry burned beneath the rubble of the train wreck. Kenosis is very real. Resilience is real. Praise God! I sustained just enough of what I called "a want to" for the Holy Spirit to work through. I found God's grace simply astounding, for He still wanted to use me when I felt inadequate and unworthy. Sometimes I felt the need to decline ministry invitations to protect God's people from my holy mess. Each time I fixed my lips to say, "No, I cannot accommodate your request this time; however, please keep me in mind," the Holy Spirit would rise within, take over my tongue and say, "Yes, yes, yes." To my humble astonishment, I discovered that I had a built-in reserve labeled, "I can do all things" (Philippians 4:13).

I found His grace profoundly amazing: He used me the most when I was weakest. During this season of spiritual blindness, when I sank deep in sin far from the peaceful shores, God compassionately threw me a life preserver ring. The red lettering on the ring displayed 2 Corinthians 12:9–10, which was guaranteed to get my attention: This time, He encouraged me to shift the focus from the "sufficient grace" portion to the "power of Christ resting upon me" aspect. What a revelation! Settling down with the resting part was still a long, arduous journey, and I faltered at least 1,000 times.

Nevertheless, God always proved Himself able to save. He was determined to *help* get me up off the ground and into the air where I belonged. He lovingly worked around my fumbles and blunders. Like any good father regarding His child, I am sure He must have often felt exasperated with me, yet His love never wavered.

*Holy Spirit
needs "a want to"
to work
through.*

decided
adjective
de·cid·ed

1: UNQUESTIONABLE

2: free from doubt or wavering[1]

CHAPTER 11

DECIDED: I THINK
I CAN TOO

In a previous chapter, I shared the nursery rhyme,

> Humpty Dumpty sat on a wall,
> Humpty Dumpty had a great fall.
> All the king's horses and all the king's men
> Couldn't put Humpty together again.[2]

I said I had also fallen and felt unable to get up again. Sisters, the good news is that the bad news wasn't true because my thoughts finally received an upgrade! Instead of Humpty's story, I chose to courageously echo the sentiments of another beloved childhood story called *The Little Engine That Could*. Despite its insecurities about its size when it compared itself to the larger, more powerful trains, the little engine took on an assignment and decided to give itself a chance, saying, *"I—think—I—can, I—think—I—can."* It *REACHED THE TOP by drawing on bravery and then went on down the grade, congratulating itself by saying, "I thought I could, I thought I could."[3]*

That little blue train was determined to view getting up that hill as a blessing and gave it his best shot. When I was sick and tired of being sick and tired, I grabbed hold of determination. My mind needed to be transformed because I was living way beneath my potential and kingdom inheritance (Romans 12:2). I looked at myself in the mirror and made a decision. I decided I also had what it took to get to the top because my engine was powered, not by steam, but by the Holy Ghost. I decided my purpose was worth pursuing even if it continued to take a lot. Kathryn Kuhlman, one of my healing ministry sheroes, once said of the anointing, "It'll cost you everything, absolutely everything."[4]

Yes, the cost preceded my birth (Jeremiah 1:5), and I decided to rise from my ashes, accepting that I could not change what was or was not. I made the decision to no longer hold on to a woe-is-me victimized persona but to participate in intentional positive growth opportunities through every means possible.

Over the decades, those avenues included receiving salvation, connecting with a Word-based church, activating the Holy Spirit, studying the Bible, fasting, and attending life and spiritual enrichment workshops. Additionally, I've read hundreds of books on faith, healing, and deliverance in overcoming trauma. I've also watched 1,000 videos on intention, vision, and purpose.

Moreover, I have attended countless conferences across regions on understanding the Godkind of faith that will grant access to miracles.

As I searched for my true identity within myself, one of the first lessons I learned as a human service counselor stuck in my mind: "If the ones who were supposed to love and care for you didn't do it, shame on them. Shame on *you* if you let it ruin the rest of your life." I decided to RISE above all the shameful moments because those moments were not who I *was*; they were what I had experienced.

My decision to accept God's promises led me to take accountability for, ownership of, and responsibility for areas I struggled in. My decision to become free came from my realizing I deserved it, so I began the heart work to push past the pain. I stopped invalidating and devaluing myself in comparison to others. I stopped letting the enemy use my mind as a garbage dump for evil, nonproductive thoughts.

Despite how long I have taken to make it to this moment, I've decided to shut down the adopted imposter syndrome and vet the true, authentic ME like never before. I've decided to get to know who I authentically AM. I've decided to embrace or reject thought processes and responses as needed. As I evolve into a better version of myself, it has become my priority to love myself just as I am.

I prioritize caring for my mental, emotional, physical, and spiritual health. For this reason, mindfulness about my relationships with others and myself is necessary.

I decided long ago to stop wanting to have honey-colored or caramel-colored skin and to embrace my special dark chocolate complexion. I decided to stop trying to lower my preaching pitch and avoid being so loud because I was created to bring the noise for the cause of Christ, especially after all that He had brought me through. I decided to stop trying to be popular on social media and to accept that I am not for everybody and that is OK. I decided to replace negative speech and learned behavior with positive speech and learned behavior since what I "[thought] in my heart" (Proverbs 23:7) always became my reality. I decided to drive my reality instead of letting my reality drive me.

I made many keen decisions, but they had three primary anchors. The first was that God expected me to steward my life to the best of my ability (Matthew 25: 14–30). Second, I finally agreed with God's decision that I was special. Third, I owed myself the satisfaction of leaving this life empty, not full.

In the introduction, I told you what I would say if I could talk with my younger self. I would also tell Jackie Denise that letting go and letting God have His way has resulted in a new trajectory that I couldn't have achieved on my own. I believe that despite my adverse childhood experiences, trauma, and drama, I am an amazing, beautiful, intelligent, kind, loving, loveable, and anointed "Somebody." I am not just anybody but a living example of grace, mercy, and favor. I am proof that God can transform a broken, defeated life from the inside out. I am destined to make an unforgettable impact on women's lives worldwide by promoting the power of an elevated mindset like that of the little engine who thought he could—and so he did (Psalm 27:13).

I'm here, & I've got what it takes to rise to the top.

delivered
transitive verb
de·liv·ered

3 a (1): to assist (a pregnant female) in giving birth
(2): to aid in the birth of
b: to give birth to
c: to cause (oneself) to produce
as if by giving birth[1]

CHAPTER 12

DELIVERED: MY "USED TO" IS NO LONGER TRUE

The moment a baby enters the world, it requires immediate attention. Back in the day, as soon as a baby was delivered through the birth canal, a doctor used to slap its bottom to make it cry. When done properly, the doctor's action may seem harsh, but clearing the baby's lungs and airways of any mucus or fluid accumulated inside the womb is necessary. The baby also had to receive a thorough cleaning to remove all the nasty gunk it had collected while growing and developing inside the womb. Though technically delivered, the baby only received a thumbs-up after hospital staff or midwives were satisfied with the examination processes.

Slowly but surely, God's grace has subjected me to a thorough exam. With the help of a few assigned angels along the way, I made it back from every dark season safe and in my right mind.

Did you hear that? I made it back from the brink of insanity. I made it back from the tentacles of death. I made it back from a bruised, crushed spirit. I made it back from unhealthy "I messages" that shot blazing arrows straight into the recesses of my brain. I made it back from a torrent of shotgun shells aimed at taking my life with one pull of the trigger. I made it back from the ravages of self-imposed spiritual blindness. God kept a close eye on my life and helped me make it back from EVERYTHING that had tried to destroy me.

I've found that what didn't—no, *couldn't*—kill me only made me stronger. The enemy laughed gleefully at the thought that the few encounters I dared to share—there were many more— would surely crush me. And they almost did, but God would not allow it. Christ completely confounded the enemy by transforming the crushed olives into 100% extra virgin olive oil. I am so oily that if you walk behind me, you might slide right down! No adverse childhood experience, drama, or trauma has been without purpose. I do not despise any of it because all of it has made me who I am today. Despite vicious accusers within and without, the Lord was my faithful defender (Deuteronomy 20:4). His steadfast love *willed me to rise*, stand, and climb.

Several years ago, I was answering questions about myself during a stroll around town. My date listened attentively to every word I said. As soon as I finished sharing, Tracy surprised me by asking, "Jackie, do you realize that you often use the phrase 'I used to' when talking about yourself?" As I nodded, I was speechless; it had never occurred to me. However, it immediately resonated with me, revealing that I had been mentally and emotionally stuck in a losing season. That surprising yet insightful revelation helped me decide to get unstuck. You're probably thinking, "Uh, that sounds good, but *how* did you get unstuck?"

There is a simple yet profound answer: Not long ago, I got tired of doing the same things and getting the same underwhelming results. I got tired enough to course-correct by getting quiet and examining myself with a more powerful telescope with no blind spots. Looking through that telescope, I began considering my life experiences, trauma, and drama. Like a person searching for an object within an optical illusion, I looked deep within to find common threads. The thickest, most undeniable thread was the need to be loved, with the need for personal safety running a close second. The third runner-up was the need for cleansing to eliminate pride-fueled shame. I had to recognize these needs and recalibrate my mindset about every adverse childhood experience, drama, and trauma I had ever experienced. Once I was at peace with every encounter, I began to move forward. Over time, I moved from thinking to believing to KNOWING that I was predestined to survive life's train wrecks and thrive despite them.

Today, my "used to" is no longer true. I am no longer trapped and held hostage by destructive thoughts telling me that I'm not good enough, strong enough, or popular enough. According to Proverbs 23:7, *"as a man thinks in his heart, so is he."* This has become infinitely more real to me. The things that once appeared incredibly catastrophic to me, I now view closely through a higher-quality telescope's field of vision. In this more conscious mindset, I can no longer afford to think as I used to about people, places, and things. The limited thinking I used to have did not serve me well, so I have changed it with God's help.

Despite my growth, I do not claim to have "arrived," but I know I'm on my way. Here are some daily confessions that help me stay elevated so that I can effectively assist others:

- ~ The Holy Spirit fills and guides me every day!
- ~ I have been given something powerful to say that has influence!
- ~ The Lord will perfect everything that concerns me!
- ~ Jesus is the center of my joy, and that joy is my strength!
- ~ I am full of GOD-fidence and my OWN courageous confidence!
- ~ I am cheerful and speak words that create wonders in my life!
- ~ Amazing things happen daily to, in, for, and around me!
- ~ The power of God rests upon me, and I act like I believe it!
- ~ I will start again and not stop until I am proud!
- ~ I am determined and see victory in the end!

My new identity and story are in divine alignment with these sample confessions. Every setback, whether long ago or recently, has been an opportunity for a comeback. Previously, I said you could say my name was "Chosen." Well, feel free to also call me "Comeback Jack!" It feels good because where I am is no longer where I've been and what I used to do is no longer what I still do. I'm focusing and concentrating on where I'm going. It is a momentous time in my life, and I intend to rise to the occasion to receive what I have not seen or heard (1 Corinthians 2:9).

Despite my having a colorful past filled with a dimension of brokenness that often took my breath away, none of it has ruined me. Adverse childhood experiences, drama, and unexpected trauma tried hard to silence my voice but failed! Although it has been tough, I firmly believe in faith, grace, and possibilities because I have received them in abundance. My assignment, my mission is to advance God's Kingdom by building up broken women. I've already ministered healing and deliverance to thousands of souls, directly and indirectly, and at least one million more are waiting.

Destiny knows my full name and keeps calling me because the call is bigger than me. It has always been bigger than me because it includes you. Remember how I asked God where the icing on my cake was? I discovered that what I thought was missing was never missing at all. Destiny was always inside me, waiting for me to rise and recognize that *I was* my icing. Lord have mercy!

There's even a juicy black cherry on top: I just heard the Holy Spirit whisper, "For your faithfulness, I'm giving you beauty for ashes" (Isaiah 61:3).

Once again, I am blinking back tears of gratitude. Why? It is because God does not measure faithfulness as we do. The enemy tried to defeat me by torturing my internal belief system so I would never rise to my full potential. Low self-esteem, self-confidence, and self-image caused me to count myself out many times. Thankfully, God corrected my math every time and added me right back in. Due to His favor-filled calculations, I was no longer damaged goods with broken, scattered parts inside that couldn't be repaired.

God has always had a sovereign plan. Microwave moments have been few; oven experiences have been more common. Just as that delicious pound cake with the icing drizzled over it has to slow bake until it's ready, so it has been with me. Yes, indeed, thoughts of defeat that engulfed my mindset from pre-womb exposure were slowly but surely replaced with positive self-efficacy. Since I deepened my introspection, embraced the necessary heart work, and reset my attitude, my confidence has grown daily (Philippians 4:13).

Although I am not the first woman to face challenging situations in her life, heartache and pain know me quite intimately. My life began haphazardly; I have hurt and cried a lot, but that doesn't matter anymore. Upon reflection, I see God has always been with me, fighting for me in every chapter of my life. Destiny would not let me succumb to attacks or poor choices. It continues to whisper, "Rise, Jackie, rise. Believe in yourself and rise no matter what!" Regardless of its source, no sorrow has been wasted. Because I have overcome everything that has tried to overcome me, I am not a victim but a victor.

This overcomer status includes an encounter that happened quite unexpectedly today. Having waited near the entranceway of the church for my family to prepare for the transition from my cousin's homegoing service to the committal site, I turned around, expecting to assess the remaining wait time. Instead, I found myself looking directly into the face of the woman who babysat and molested me twice when I lived in Richardson Courts in Nashville, North Carolina, as a child. At the tender age of 8 years or so, I was instructed to sit still on her lap and be quiet while she violated my innocence. She told me not to tell anyone because I would get into big trouble, so I didn't tell.

I had buried that memory and never spoke of it to anyone until I confided in my therapist three days after crossing paths with the woman. In the first observation, I could see that she instantly recognized me when we locked eyes, and she remembered what she had done to me when she was a teen. Second, I realized that seeing her did not hurt me at all. Glory, glory, and glory! I remained calm. Having worked in human services and mental health, I know the far-reaching effects of child molestation. I realized she might have been a victim of this at some point in her own childhood.

I calmly walked to Blackberry, my 2018 Nissan Kicks, and slowly slid into the soft, cushioned seat with light gray embroidered stitching. While absentmindedly gliding my hands around the steering wheel perimeter, I wondered what seeing her meant. What the what?! Why had I come face to face with her after all these years? Why today, when I am planning to put the final touches on this closing chapter of my manuscript once I return home in a couple of hours? Silently I watched the woman from across the parking lot for about 3 minutes. As I surveyed her appearance from head to toe, I noticed she wasn't aging well and looked sad from the inside out. Perhaps I was viewing her through the eyes and adolescent mindset of an innocent 8-year-old.

Momentarily, it felt like I was about to be snatched back to that space in time. Shaking my head from side to side, I disallowed that trip down trauma lane by speaking the Word out loud. I took authority over my mindset and commanded myself to rise above this unexpected encounter. Deep down, I knew it was a desperate, last-ditch blunt force strike meant to test whether a trauma bond still existed. Satan had hit me with a sucker punch to see if he had the power to set me back emotionally and psychologically. He intended to play with my mind and emotions but only played himself. It was too late for his plan because I was delivered from that adverse childhood experience. I discovered that I had been protected from it for years by a Wakanda-like forcefield (Psalm 51:12). I saw the airstrike in living color as it came for me; however, I did not feel it.

After I had sat down to wait for my family, I instinctively opened my Samsung Note 9 Android mobile phone to take a picture of her full body. I used my thumb and forefinger to zoom in on her profile to study her photo up close. Just as I was about to press that dime-sized, white button at the bottom of the screen, I heard the Holy Spirit whisper, "Don't put that photo in your phone and don't carry it home with you. Forgive her." My face wrinkled as I threw my head back and released a deep breath.

The spot where the woman stood in the parking lot positioned her right on my side of the vehicle. I moved Blackberry's gear from the park position to drive and slowly passed by the woman. Although I was no more than 5 feet away; it never crossed my mind to run her over, back up, and repeat. My head never turned to the left or right. I didn't glance into the side-view mirror, and there was zero need to look into the rear windshield mirror. Genuinely and authentically, I said aloud, "I forgive you."

Now more than ever, I know destiny helpers have worked long and hard with me to clean up my train tracks, and no debris has been left behind. Without my knowledge, the clean-up had graciously included a situation I had buried for 45 years. I have experienced far more than I can share in this one volume of work, but I am not discouraged or dismayed in the slightest, for it has all been part of my life's learning curve. What matters now is that there is a new train ticket tucked in the inside zipper compartment of my tan and salmon-colored crossbody Coach bag. I'm riding the right train with a heavenly-certified train conductor, so I'll be fine. Rather than freaking out about my future, I am at peace. I know the continued journey will take as long as it takes, but I'm built for it. Thankfully, there's not only a new path but also an improved pathology. The process involves overcoming deep insecurities, anxiety, and negative mental conditioning. Doing so will allow me to exercise greater emotional intelligence and stop ignoring obvious red flags regarding people, places, and things as I move forward in life.

Having a positive mindset is everything! I keep shifting mine UP because that's where *Destiny Keeps Calling Me.* I completely trust this driver and the destination. I am not worried about seeing myself behind bars for life when we come to a stop. Due to a newly discovered narrative, I feel free and look forward to the rest of my life being the best it has ever been based on Amos 9:13–14: *"Yes indeed, it won't be long now."* God's Decree. *"Things are going to happen so fast your head will swim, one thing fast on the heels of the other. You won't be able to keep up. Everything will be happening at once—and everywhere you look, blessings! Blessings like wine pouring off the mountains and hills."*

Regardless of adverse childhood experiences, trauma, and drama, God has never turned His back on me, for He has always known my end. The enemy has been all up, in, and through my excessive train wrecks; he gloated over the smoldering smoke. Satan, however, forgot that where there is smoke, there is fire, so GOD still got all the glory. An epic destiny is gingerly unfolding before my eyes like the pointed petals of a blood-orange tulip, my favorite flower. Without fear but with hands raised in the air—*as if* I were on a tall roller coaster—I am screaming with childlike anticipation and giddy, uncontainable delight: "Ok, Daddy-God, Let's go!"

*God knows
the end
from the
beginning.*

Conclusion

Today, I was asked, "Why do you want the world to know about your private business?" I remained silent instead of responding. I heard a voice speak the answer in that silent space, reminding me that I was chosen and anointed for transparency to set others free. God chose me to impart post-traumatic wisdom to women who lacked self-worth and value due to a lack of healthy love that they could feel and see. He told me to show my scars because they signified where excruciating fresh wounds *"used to be."*

God's beauty and love have followed after me every day of my life (Psalm 23:6). Consequently, I have been given a powerful mindset message to motivate, inspire, and transform lives. When women worldwide examine their whole life narrative—not just the highlights—and tell themselves the truth, the whole truth, and nothing but the truth, they can rise above life's train wrecks. Rejecting shame or regret, they can confidently move forward without giving a flip about what anyone other than God thinks about their destiny course.

"Blessed is she who falls down.
Blessed is she who rises again."
~Birds of Paradise, Movie

NOTES

Chapter 1

1. *Merriam-Webster*, s.v. "train wreck," accessed February 18, 2021, https://www.merriam-webster.com/dictionary/train wreck.

2. *Merriam-Webster*, s.v. "destined," accessed March 18, 2022, https://www.merriam-webster.com/dictionary/destined.

Chapter 2

1. *Merriam-Webster*, s.v. "deserted," accessed February 18, 2021, https://www.merriam-webster.com/dictionary/deserted.

2. Marty, Jonathan: The Story of the Bronx's Spofford Juvenile Detention Center https://urbandemos.nyu.edu/2018/05/23.

Chapter 3

1. *Merriam-Webster*, s.v. "debilitated," accessed April 5, 2021, https://www.merriam-webster.com/dictionary/debilitated.

2. Mayo Staff Clinic: Guillain-Barré Syndrome, https://www.mayoclinic.org/diseases-conditions, accessed April 5, 2021.

Chapter 4

1. *Merriam-Webster*, s.v. "destroyed," accessed March 25, 2021, https://www.merriam-webster.com/dictionary/destroyed.

Chapter 5

1. *Merriam-Webster*, s.v. "devastated," accessed March 25, 2021, https://www.merriam-webster.com/dictionary/devastated.

Chapter 6

1. *Merriam-Webster*, s.v. "demoralized," accessed May 15, 2021, https://www.merriam-webster.com/dictionary/demoralized.

Chapter 7

1. *Merriam-Webster*, s.v. "deployed," accessed May 27, 2021, https://www.merriam-webster.com/dictionary/deployed.
2. https://yourzengrowth.com/how-to-bloom-where-youre-planted/, accessed March 19, 202 2.

Chapter 8

1. *Merriam-Webster*, s.v. "denied," accessed April 22, 2022, https://www.merriam-webster.com/dictionary/denied.
2. https://www.lyrics.com/lyric/16559960/Bill+Withers/Ain%27t+No+Sunshine, "Ain't No Sunshine Lyrics." *Lyrics.com*. STANDS4 LLC, accessed September 20, 2022.

Chapter 9

1. *Merriam-Webster*, s.v. "derailed," accessed April 5, 2021, https://www.merriam-webster.com/dictionary/derailed.

2. https://allnurseryrhymes.com/humpty-dumpty/, accessed November 10, 2021.

Chapter 10

1. *Merriam-Webster*, s.v. "defeated," accessed June 16, 2021, https://www.merriam-webster.com/dictionary/defeated.

2. https://www.goodreads.com/quotes/420478-the-only-thing-worse-than-being-blind-is-having-sight, Helen Keller.

Chapter 11

1. *Merriam-Webster*, s.v. "decided," accessed August 8, 2022, https://www.merriam-webster.com/dictionary/decided.

2. https://allnurseryrhymes.com/humpty-dumpty/, accessed November 10, 2021.

3. Piper, Watty. (2001). The Little Engine That Could. G.P. Putnam's Sons. https://littleengine.fandom.com/wiki/The_Little_Engine_That_Could_(book).

4. https://idoc.pub/documents/kathryn-kuhlman-a-spiritual-biography-of-gods-miracle-working-power-6klzj6ex1qng.

Chapter 12

1. *Merriam-Webster*, s.v. "delivered," accessed February 18, 2021, https://www.merriam-webster.com/dictionary/delivered.

Acknowledgments

Many have left indelible impressions on my heart, mind, and spirit throughout my life. With great gratitude, I thank the following people for helping me create this particular assignment:

~ Accountability Birthing Coach Kimberly Holmes, for nine months, you collaborated with me virtually every week, helping me give birth to the words in my belly. Afterward, there were still areas to clean up, but my book baby had been born. You pushed me to get this manuscript out of my head and into the world so that it could honor God, me, and others. You held my feet to the fire, periodically cracked the whip, and assertively said on more than one occasion without even blinking, "Just write!" You did not relent when tears of frustration and excuses flowed from my swollen eyelids. In a voice that sounded just like God's, you said, "I see a brave, bold, and beautiful soul willing to fearlessly be an open book to assist others through their deliverance processes. Jackie, finish what you have started."

~ Introspective Coach Tanika Martin, you challenged me to rest and rid myself of limiting beliefs and behaviors. You reminded me of my spoken mantra, "Movement inspires movement." Hearing my words echoed back to me held me accountable for my actions and motivated me to continue pursuing my purpose. You encouraged me to trust GOD instead of outside anchors and to allow HIM to adjust my sails. You challenged me to "relinquish control and let it FLOW!" Having faith in me, you said, "Jackie, with radical confidence, you are destined to become like a dancing airman balloon that flies freely under the direction of the wind." With the strength of a quiet storm, you commanded me to unlock my gifts, activate my courage, and soar.

Made in the USA
Middletown, DE
08 February 2023

24388552R00106